Haskell Financial Data Modeling and Predictive Analytics

Get an in-depth analysis of financial time series from the perspective of a functional programmer

Pavel Ryzhov

[PACKT] open source
community experience distilled
PUBLISHING

BIRMINGHAM - MUMBAI

Haskell Financial Data Modeling and Predictive Analytics

First published: October 2013

Production Reference: 1221013

Published by Packt Publishing Ltd.
Livery Place
35 Livery Street
Birmingham B3 2PB, UK..

ISBN 978-1-78216-943-7

www.packtpub.com

Cover Image by Duraid Fatouhi (duraidfatouhi@yahoo.com)

Credits

Author
Pavel Ryzhov

Reviewers
Gregory Collins
Ivan Perez

Acquisition Editor
Sam Birch

Commissioning Editor
Harsha Bharwani

Technical Editors
Krishnaveni Haridas
Chandni Maishery

Project Coordinator
Joel Goveya

Proofreader
Clyde Jenkns

Indexer
Tejal Soni

Graphics
Ronak Dhruv

Production Coordinator
Nilesh R. Mohite

Cover Work
Nilesh R. Mohite

About the Author

Pavel Ryzhov has graduated from the Lomonosov Moscow State University in Russia in the field of mathematical physics, Toda equations and Lie algebras. In the past 10 years, he has worked as a Technical Lead and Senior Software Engineer. In the last three years, Pavel lead a startup company that mainly provided mathematical and web software development in Haskell. Also, he works on port of Quantlib, an HQuantLib project in his spare time.

I would like personally to thank my wife Marina and daughter Marta for supporting my beginnings, my parents for encouraging me, and the enormously helpful Haskell community for providing the best tools in the world.

About the Reviewers

Gregory Collins is a software engineer at Google Zürich, where he works on web search indexing. He has done M.Sc. in Computer Science from the Yale University, and has been programming in Haskell for over a decade.

Ivan Perez has been passionate about programming and mathematics since he was seven years old. He first learned Basic and Logo, which allowed him to experiment with basic programs and computer graphics. After using Visual Basic for several years, he went to a university, where he started programming in many other languages, including Ada, Prolog, and Haskell. This changed his view of software development forever, and he decided to focus on functional and logic programming in his career.

He obtained the degree of engineering in Computer Science from the Technical University of Madrid (UPM) in 2008, and a master's degree in Computational Logic in 2009 from the same university. He collaborated and worked with the Babel Research Group at UPM from 2003 to 2010, and worked for IMDEA Software from 2007 to 2009. In 2012, he also worked for the **High Performance Computing Center (HLRS)** at the University of Stuttgart, as part of a research project involving functional programming and supercomputing.

He is the founder of Keera Studios (now Keera Studios Ltd.), a UK-based company that uses Haskell, Scala, and other cool languages to create desktop, mobile, and web applications, and games.

I would like to thank the author, the editors, and the people at Packt for making this book possible. I would like to thank my wife, Natalia for her constant support and love, and my family and friends for always being there. I would also like to thank my associates and colleagues, who had the patience to listen to my crazy ideas and to embark with me on some of them. And last, but not the least, I would like to thank all the clients and companies who took a leap of faith with functional programming, and the whole Haskell community who made working with this language the most joyful experience.

---

www.PacktPub.com

Support files, eBooks, discount offers and more

You might want to visit www.PacktPub.com for support files and downloads related to your book.

Did you know that Packt offers eBook versions of every book published, with PDF and ePub files available? You can upgrade to the eBook version at www.PacktPub.com and as a print book customer, you are entitled to a discount on the eBook copy. Get in touch with us at service@packtpub.com for more details.

At www.PacktPub.com, you can also read a collection of free technical articles, sign up for a range of free newsletters and receive exclusive discounts and offers on Packt books and eBooks.

PACKTLIB

http://PacktLib.PacktPub.com

Do you need instant solutions to your IT questions? PacktLib is Packt's online digital book library. Here, you can access, read and search across Packt's entire library of books.

Why Subscribe?

- Fully searchable across every book published by Packt
- Copy and paste, print and bookmark content
- On demand and accessible via web browser

Free Access for Packt account holders

If you have an account with Packt at www.PacktPub.com, you can use this to access PacktLib today and view nine entirely free books. Simply use your login credentials for immediate access.

Table of Contents

Preface

Welcome to *Haskell Financial Data Modeling and Predictive Analytics*. You will start with the most distinctive features of the language, then go through the data collection process with parsing, cleansing and archiving, and then come directly to data analysis and manipulation. You will learn a set of basic financial models that are commonly used in the industry and how they can be implemented in Haskell. At the end of the book you will learn deterministic parallelism and compiler-driven stream fusion optimization.

What this book covers

Chapter 1, Getting Started with the Haskell Platform, discusses a little bit of Haskell history, how to get the Haskell platform installed, and walks through a quick tour of the main features of the language.

Chapter 2, Getting your Hands Dirty, covers the first step of any data analytics project; that is, getting an input data into an appropriate database. You will learn how to write parsers in combinator style, how to work with databases by means of Persistent ORM, and how to establish outlier detection procedures to cut off erroneous data.

Chapter 3, Measuring Tick Intervals, is the most mathematical chapter, as you will learn point processes that are models of orders arriving from exchanges. It also covers the property-based test framework, QuickCheck.

Chapter 4, Going Autoregressive, covers a classical autoregressive model of intertick duration, and finds out how to use Haskell stream fusion to achieve near-C performance of the calibration code.

Chapter 5, Volatility, covers one of the most successful volatility model of financial mathematics–Generalized Autoregressive Conditional Heteroskedasticity. Haskell's approach to parallel computations is explained, and a divide-and-conquer metaalgorithm is shown in practice.

Chapter 6, Advanced Cabal, explains the main approach to packaging, building, and maintaining dependencies of Haskell projects.

Appendix, References, contains references for the topics in the book, and explains them in greater details.

What you need for this book

In order to run most of the examples in this book you will need only Windows, Linux, or Mac OS X installed. All the needed software will be installed with the Haskell platform installer.

For *Chapter 2, Getting your Hands Dirty*, you will need an installation of one of the RDBMS: Sqlite, MySql, PostgreSQL, MongoDB, or CouchDB.

Who this book is for

Developers who are working in finance and would like to know how functional programming might be applied in the area will find this book of great use. Preliminary knowledge of Haskell is welcomed but is not required.

Conventions

In this book, you will find a number of styles of text that distinguish between different kinds of information. Here are some examples of these styles, and an explanation of their meaning.

Code words in text are shown as follows: "The trace of the program is written into the `.tix` files."

A block of code is set as follows:

```
parProduct :: Num a => [a] -> a
parProduct [] = 1
parProduct [x] = x
parProduct xs = (right `using` rpar) * left
    where
        n = length xs `div` 2
        (leftL, rightL) = splitAt n xs
        left = product leftL
        right = product rightL
```

When we wish to draw your attention to a particular part of a code block, the relevant lines or items are set in bold:

```
[default]
exten => s,1,Dial(Zap/1|30)
exten => s,2,Voicemail(u100)
exten => s,102,Voicemail(b100)
exten => i,1,Voicemail(s0)
```

Any command-line input or output is written as follows:

```
$ ./QuickTestsFull
+++ OK, passed 100 tests.
+++ OK, passed 100 tests.
+++ OK, passed 100 tests.
+++ OK, passed 100 tests.
```

New terms and **important words** are shown in bold. Words that you see on the screen, in menus or dialog boxes for example, appear in the text like this: "clicking on the **Next** button moves you to the next screen".

> Warnings or important notes appear in a box like this.

> Tips and tricks appear like this.

Reader feedback

Feedback from our readers is always welcome. Let us know what you think about this book—what you liked or may have disliked. Reader feedback is important for us to develop titles that you really get the most out of.

To send us general feedback, simply send an e-mail to `feedback@packtpub.com`, and mention the book title via the subject of your message.

If there is a topic that you have expertise in and you are interested in either writing or contributing to a book, see our author guide on `www.packtpub.com/authors`.

Customer support

Now that you are the proud owner of a Packt book, we have a number of things to help you to get the most from your purchase.

Downloading the example code

You can download the example code files for all Packt books you have purchased from your account at `http://www.packtpub.com`. If you purchased this book elsewhere, you can visit `http://www.packtpub.com/support` and register to have the files e-mailed directly to you.

Errata

Although we have taken every care to ensure the accuracy of our content, mistakes do happen. If you find a mistake in one of our books—maybe a mistake in the text or the code—we would be grateful if you would report this to us. By doing so, you can save other readers from frustration and help us improve subsequent versions of this book. If you find any errata, please report them by visiting `http://www.packtpub.com/submit-errata`, selecting your book, clicking on the **errata submission form** link, and entering the details of your errata. Once your errata are verified, your submission will be accepted and the errata will be uploaded on our website, or added to any list of existing errata, under the Errata section of that title. Any existing errata can be viewed by selecting your title from `http://www.packtpub.com/support`.

Piracy

Piracy of copyright material on the Internet is an ongoing problem across all media. At Packt, we take the protection of our copyright and licenses very seriously. If you come across any illegal copies of our works, in any form, on the Internet, please provide us with the location address or website name immediately so that we can pursue a remedy.

Please contact us at `copyright@packtpub.com` with a link to the suspected pirated material.

We appreciate your help in protecting our authors, and our ability to bring you valuable content.

Questions

You can contact us at `questions@packtpub.com` if you are having a problem with any aspect of the book, and we will do our best to address it.

1
Getting Started with the Haskell Platform

The first version of Haskell was standardized in 1990. After a series of intermediate standards, the minimal, stable, and portable version of the language was published as "The Haskell 98 Report" in February 1999. This successful standard was revised in 2003 and published as "Haskell 98 Language and Libraries: The Revised Report". This is the most supported version of the language and it is implemented in many compilers and interpreters of Haskell. The latest specification, Haskell 2010, adds **Foreign Function Interface** (**FFI**) for binding to other programming languages, fixes some syntax issues, and introduces several pluggable language extensions. Throughout this book, we will use Haskell 2010.

So what is Haskell? It is a fast, type-safe, purely functional programming language with a powerful type inference. Having said that, let us try to understand what it gives us.

First, a purely functional programming language means that, in general, functions in Haskell don't have side effects. There is a special type for impure functions, or functions with side effects.

Then, Haskell has a strong, static type system with an automatic and robust type inference. This, in practice, means that you do not usually need to specify types of functions and also the type checker does not allow passing incompatible types. In strongly typed languages, types are considered to be a specification, due to the Curry-Howard correspondence, the direct relationship between programs and mathematical proofs. Under this great simplification, the theorem states that if a value of the type exists (or is inhabited), then the corresponding mathematical proof is correct. Or jokingly saying, if a program compiles, then there is 99 percent probability that it works according to specification. Though the question if the types conform, the specification in natural language is still open; Haskell won't help you with it.

The Haskell platform

The glorious Glasgow Haskell Compilation System, or simply **Glasgow Haskell Compiler** (**GHC**), is the most widely used Haskell compiler. It is the current de facto standard. The compiler is packaged into the Haskell platform that follows Python's principle, "Batteries included". The platform is updated twice a year with new compilers and libraries. It usually includes a compiler, an interactive **Read-Evaluate-Print Loop** (**REPL**) interpreter, Haskell 98/2010 libraries (so-called Prelude) that includes most of the common definitions and functions, and a set of commonly used libraries. If you are on Windows or Mac OS X, it is strongly recommended to use prepackaged installers of the Haskell platform at `http://www.haskell.org/platform/`.

Many Linux distributions include the Haskell platform in their repositories. Though it becomes less maintained, as more and more developers tend to stay on the bleeding edge, it is better to just install the core. For instance, on Debian-based systems, you can get started by running the following command:

```
sudo apt-get install ghc cabal-install
cabal update
```

Even though Windows support is quite impressive, Linux/Mac OS X installation usually has a broader support because they include the free and complete C/C++ compiler tool chain, GCC. Although MinGW32 for Windows tries to provide such toolkit, it usually lacks a few GNU libraries to be completely compatible with the Linux environment. The missing 64-bit support on Windows might be crucial for data intensive applications. So for advanced development, you require a Unix-based machine.

For example, installation on Mac OS X 10.8 is quite straightforward and can be done as follows:

1. Install the **Command Line Tools for Xcode** package from `http://developer.apple.com` to get **GNU Compiler Chain** (**GCC**). It is required for Haskell compiler to work.
2. Download a 64-bit package of Haskell platform from `http://haskell.org`.
3. Double-click on the package and the installer appears. It warns you that the Haskell platform requires GCC. Click on **Continue**, as shown in the following screenshot:

4. The platform can be installed only for all users, so just click on **Continue**:

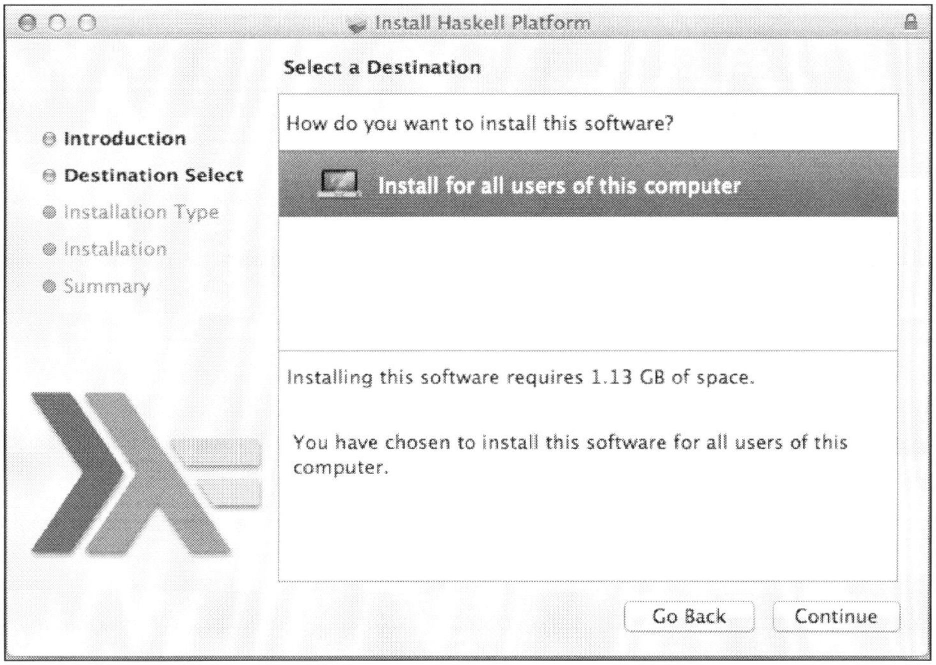

5. Now, you can modify the location of installation. However, it is recommended to leave it to default:

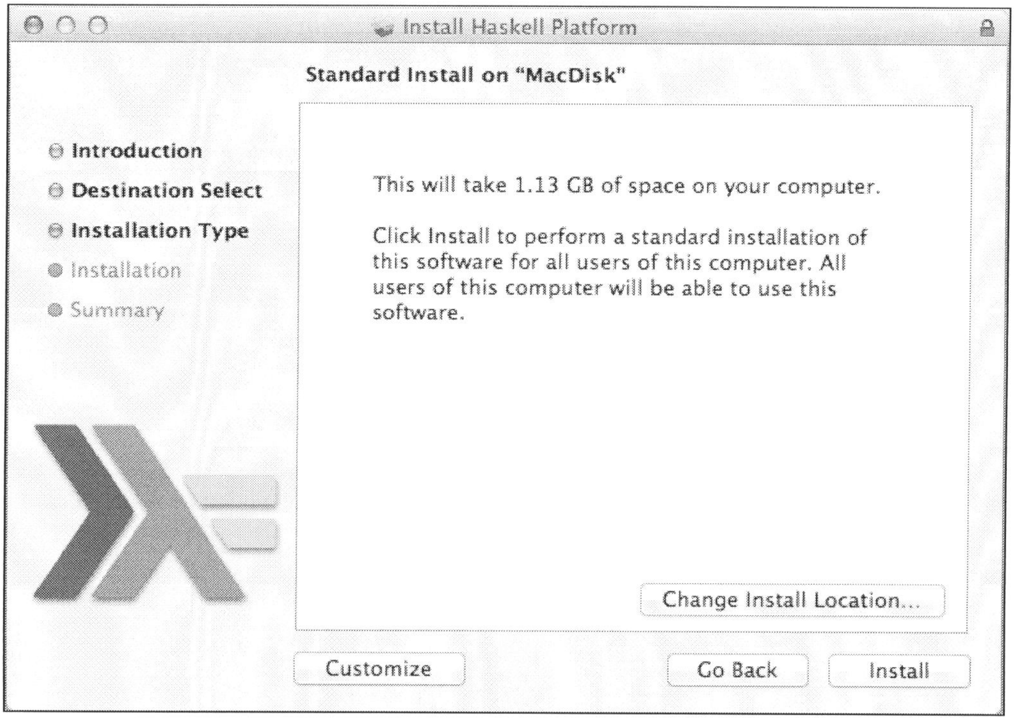

6. The installer asks for elevated credentials and you need to enter a correct password:

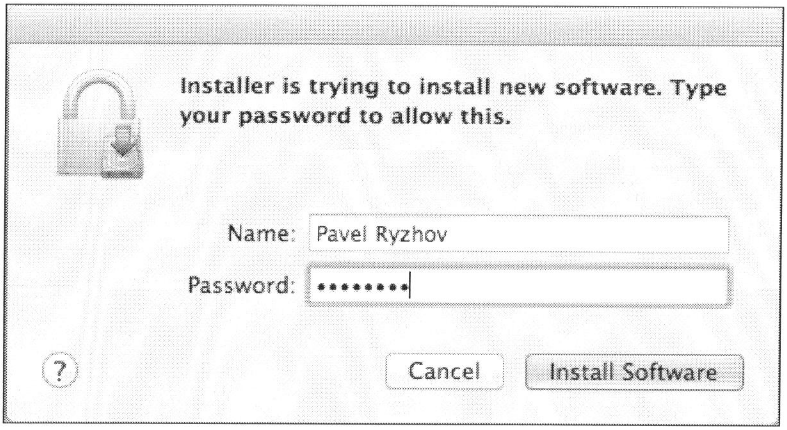

7. The platform writes a lot of files and sets up the environment:

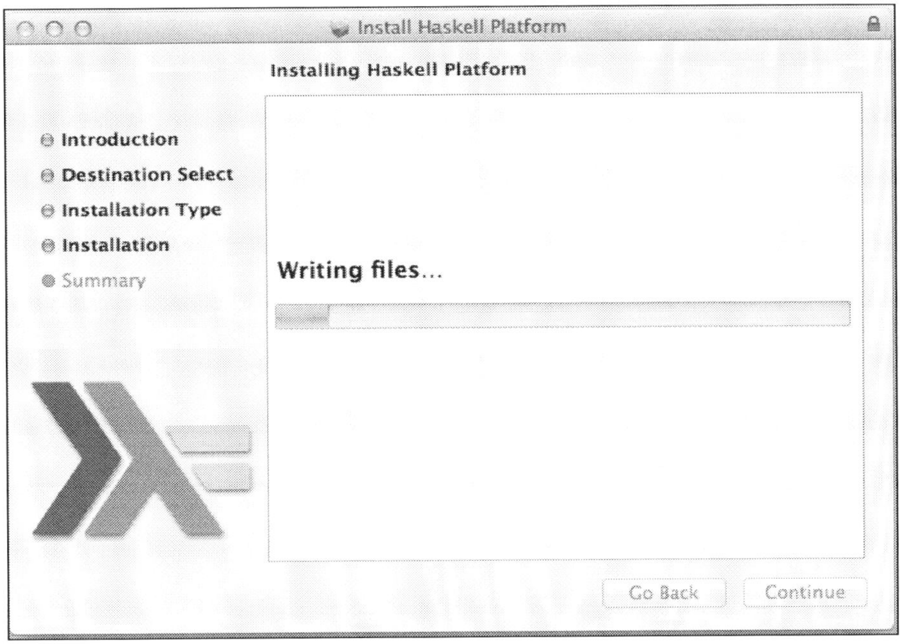

8. The installation is now complete!

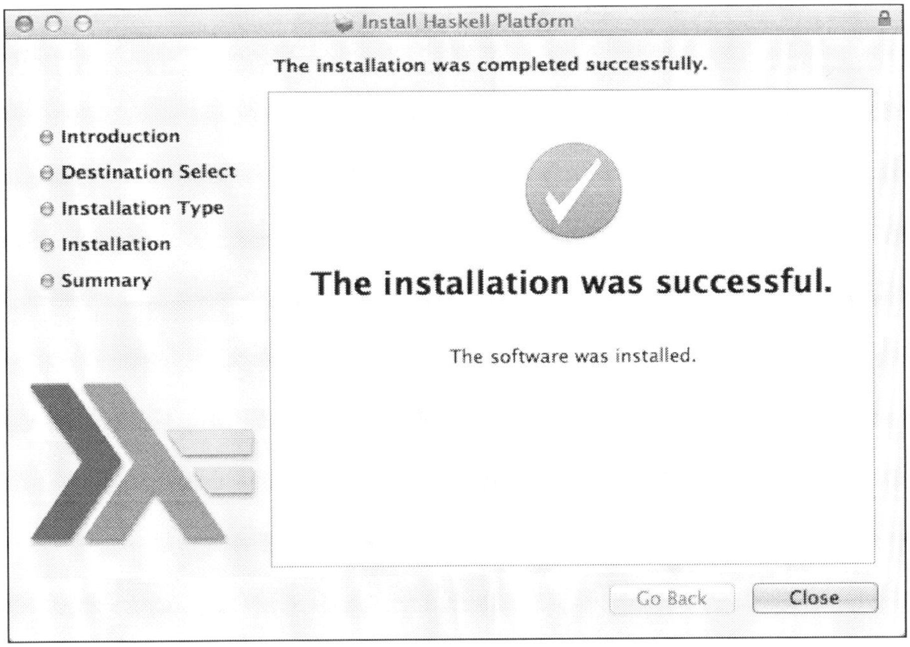

9. Now, you can try to run the Haskell interpreter by running GHCi. And if you can see something similar to the following screenshot, this installation was successful:

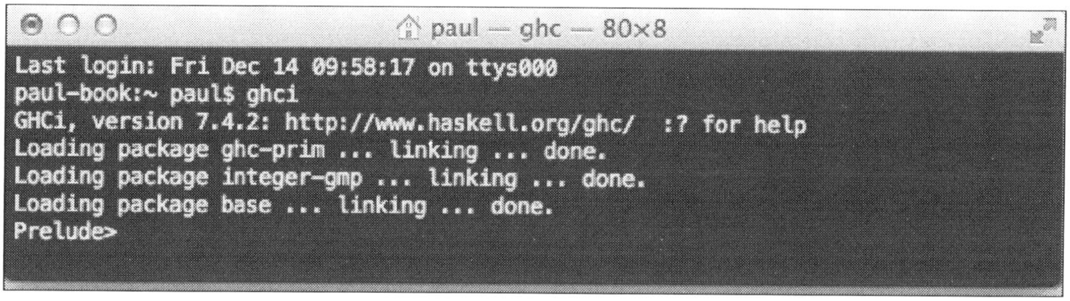

After installing it, the following tools will be available:

- The GHC compiler
- An interactive GHCi interpreter
- The packaging tool Cabal

But also you'll need a text editor. If you prefer a full-pledged IDE, then Leksah (`http://leksah.org`) might be a good choice. Otherwise, both Emacs and VIM have excellent support of Haskell including, but not limited to, syntax highlighting, code formatting, integrating with GHCi and type and tag browsers; even though, examples in this chapter require only a working interpreter.

Quick tour of Haskell

To start with development, first we should be familiar with a few basic features of Haskell. We really need to know about laziness, datatypes, pattern matching, type classes, and basic notion of monads to start with Haskell.

Laziness

Haskell is a language with lazy evaluation. From a programmer's point of view that means that the value is evaluated if and only if it is really needed. Imperative languages usually have a strict evaluation, that is, function arguments are evaluated before function application. To see the difference, let's take a look at a simple expression in Haskell:

```
let x = 2 + 3
```

In a strict or eager language, the `2 + 3` expression would be immediately evaluated to 5, whereas in Haskell, only a promise to do this evaluation will be created and the value will be evaluated only when it is needed. In other words, this statement just introduces definition of `x` which might be used afterwards, unlike in strict language where it is an operator that assigns the computed value, 5 to a memory cell named `x`. Also, this strategy allows sharing of evaluations, because laziness assumes that computations can be executed whenever it is needed and therefore, the result can be memorized. It might reduce the running time by exponential factor over strict evaluation.

Laziness also allows to manipulate with infinite data structures. For instance, we can construct an infinite list of natural numbers as follows:

```
let ns = [1..]
```

And moreover, we can manipulate it as if it is a normal list, even though some caution is needed, as you can get an infinite loop. We can take the first five elements of this infinite list by means of the built-in function, `take` as follows:

```
take 5 ns
```

By running this example in GHCi you will get `[1,2,3,4,5]`.

Functions as first-class citizens

The notion of function is one of the core ideas in functional languages and Haskell is not an exception at all. The definition of a function includes a body of function and an optional type declaration. For instance, the `take` function is defined in `Prelude` as follows:

```
take :: Int -> [a] -> [a]
take = ...
```

Here, the type declaration says that the function takes an integer as the argument and a list of objects of the `a` type, and returns a new list of the same type. Also Haskell allows partial application of a function. For example, you can construct a function that takes first five elements of the list as follows:

```
take5 :: [a] -> [a]
take5 = take 5
```

Also functions are themselves objects, that is, you may pass a function as an argument to another function. `Prelude` defines map function as a function of a function:

```
map :: (a -> b) -> [a] -> [b]
```

`map` takes a function and applies it to each element of the list. Thus functions are first-class citizens in the language and it is possible to manipulate with them as if they were normal objects.

Datatypes

Datatype is the core of a strongly-typed language as Haskell. The distinctive feature of Haskell datatypes is that they all are immutable; that is, after an object is constructed it cannot be changed. It might be weird for the first sight, but in the long run, it has several positive consequences. First, it enables computation parallelization. Second, all data is referentially transparent; that is, there is no difference between the reference to an object and the object itself. These two properties allow the compiler to reason about code optimization at a higher level than what the C/C++ compiler can.

Now, let's turn to our domain model to show how datatypes are defined in Haskell. Consider data model in a quote-driven market. The market maker posts bid and ask quotes. We can express these facts in `Quote.hs`.

The following are the three common ways to define datatypes in Haskell:

- The first declaration just creates a synonym for an existing datatype and type checker won't prevent you from using `Integer` instead of `TimeStamp`. Also, you can use a value of the `TimeStamp` type with any function that expects to work with an `Integer` datatype.
- The second declaration creates a new type for prices and you are not allowed to use `Double` instead of `Price`. The compiler will raise an error in such cases and thus it will enforce the correct usage.
- The last declaration introduces **Algebraic Data Type** (**ADT**) and says that the `Quote` type might be constructed either by the `AskQuote` data constructor, or by `BidQuote` with timestamp and price as its parameters. The `Quote` itself is called as a type constructor.

Type constructor might be parameterized by type variables. For example, the `Maybe` and `Either` types quite oftenly used standard types, and are defined in the `Quotes2.hs` file. Here, `a` and `b` are type variables; that is, any type can be placed instead of them there. The `Maybe` type is often used to represent calculation that might have ended without results. If the logarithm is defined only on the positive half of the real line, we can define a type-safe version of the logarithm function in `Log.hs`. This version will always remind you to handle the `NaN` operation in your code. What is more, the compiler will make an exhaustive check to see if all paths are covered, and it will warn you if not. Please, also note that we used a new syntactic construction, a guard, to define conditions of function application. You can use any expression evaluating to `Bool` in guards. Also, the compiler checks to see if all the right-hand definitions have the same type, even if the type is not declared explicitly. It ensures that the function type is unambiguous.

The `Either` type is commonly used for functions that can result either with an error, or with a value, and the `Right` constructor used to hold "right" values in `LogEither.hs`.

In fact, data constructors are normal functions in Haskell that return or construct a new object. If you query GHCi about type of the `Left` or `Right` constructor, it will print out the following types:

```
Prelude> :t Left
Left :: a -> Either a b
Prelude> :t Right
Right :: b -> Either a b
```

This fact allows us to pass a data constructor as the function argument, create a partially "constructed" datatype, and everything else that is possible to do with common functions in Haskell.

Type classes

Type classes in Haskell are not classes as in object-oriented languages. It is more similar to the interfaces with optional implementation. You can find them in other languages as traits, mixins, and so on but unlike in them, this feature in Haskell enables ad-hoc polymorphism; that is, a function can be applied to arguments of different types. It is also known as function overloading, or operator overloading. A polymorphic function can specify different implementation for different types.

By principle, the type class consists of function declarations over some objects. The `Eq` type class is a standard type class that specifies how to compare two objects of the same type as given in `Eq.hs`.

Here, `Eq` is the name of the type class, `a` is a type variable and `==` and `/=` are the operations defined in the type class. This definition means that some type, `a` is of `Eq` class if it has defined the `==` and `/=` operation. Moreover, the definition provides default implementation of the `/=` operation. And if you decide to implement this class for a datatype, then you need to provide single operation implementation. For example, we might make `Price` as an instance of the `Eq` type class as given in `EqPrice.hs`.

We have just defined a quite naïve implementation of the `Eq` type class. With such definition, we can start to use functions that work over any type that implements the `Eq` type class. For instance, `Prelude` has the following functions for searching in lists that rely on the implementation of `Eq`:

```
elem :: (Eq a) => a -> [a] -> Bool
notElem :: (Eq a) => a -> [a] -> Bool
lookup :: (Eq a) => a -> [(a,b)] -> Maybe b
```

The constraint `(Eq a) =>` requires the `a` type to have the `Eq` type class implemented. The first function checks if the element is in the list. The second one is a negation of an element. And the last one looks up for a key in the list of tuples. But it is important to note that type classes help to write very generic functions that work across many types just by putting a minimal required constraint on them. In object-oriented languages, it is usually implemented by interfaces, though Haskell allows you to extend library-defined datatype by implementing any type class.

There are a large number of useful type classes defined in `Prelude`. For example, `Eq` is used to define equality between two objects, `Ord` is used to specify total ordering, `Show` and `Read` are used to introduce a string representation of the object, and the `Enum` type class is used to describe enumerations, that is, datatypes with null constructors. It might be quite boring to implement this quite trivial but useful type classes for each datatype, so Haskell supports automatic derivation of most of the standard type classes. This is given in `Price.hs`.

Now, objects of the `Price` type can be converted from/to string by means of read/show functions and compared with themselves using equality operators. We will not cover all the details of the derivation. Those who want to know all the details can look them up in the Haskell language report.

Pattern matching

Pattern matching is a core feature that makes Haskell so concise and readable. In simple words, you should specify a pattern to which some input should conform and then provide implementation. Consider the classic example of factorial as given in `Pattern1.hs`.

We can see that the `factorial` function accepts objects that can be compared for equality, specified by the `Eq` type class, and are of type class `Num`, or numbers. Then, if the input is zero, the output is one. And after that for all the other inputs, the function is defined recursively, which means by itself. Recursion is an important construct in Haskell, because the language supports declarative description of computations; that is, you need to specify what should be computed but not how it should be done. That is why there is no for and while loops; you should use recursion instead of them. The compiler has optimization techniques for recursion, and it doesn't introduce a penalty that is usual for imperative languages in the form of stack overflows. Although imperative languages usually have a tail recursion optimization built into compilers, GHC supports a generalized tail recursion that covers a lot of cases. So it is usually better to pay more attention to readability and correctness of the recursion code than to achieve pure tail recursion.

The order of pattern matching is quite important; here we will explicitly state that the first rule should be used before the second. If you swap these two declarations, the compiler will display the following warning:

```
Warning: Pattern match(es) are overlapped
         In an equation for `factorial': factorial 0 = ...
```

The compiler warns you that the last pattern has been already matched by the previous declaration as given in `Pattern2.hs`.

Also the datatype structure needs to be matched. Here, we will provide a "special" treatment of zero prices and only then a standard implementation, `Pattern3.hs`.

It is also permitted to omit some parts that are not important for pattern matching, as it is done with `TimeStamp`, and it is used in nested matching for deconstructing inner datatypes.

Monads

The term **monad** comes from the category theory, which is a branch of mathematics that formalizes mathematics itself, and its concepts as a collection of objects and arrows. But from the point of view of a Haskell programmer, it is better to think of a monad as an abstract datatype that represents computation and supports common semantics. Monad defines how to chain computations of this type together. Thus, it allows a programmer to build computation pipelines to process data in steps. You can find monadic characteristics in many programming languages. Sometimes they are named as "programmable semicolons" by analogy from imperative languages, where semicolons are used to chain individual statements. The practical side of monads is that they allow to hide state. In fact, they are required only for I/O code but usage of monads simplifies a code that passes the state around. Thus, we don't need to write functions that takes input and state and returns output and, probably, the new state.

A monad contains a type constructor and two operations, `return` and bind (`>>=`). The `return` operation injects a plain value into the monad. The bind operation does the reverse process, that is, it extracts the value and passes it to the next function in the pipeline. But, it is worth mentioning that monads don't need to provide a way to get values outside them. The real-world definition of monad is extended by the fail operation and some shortcuts of the bind operation.

```
MonadPrelude.hs
```

The `Prelude` lists and `Maybe` are also monads. We can use the `Maybe` type as a primitive type of checked exception; that is, at any point if the computation fails, then the rest of computation should be skipped and return `Nothing`, otherwise, if all steps are successful, then the final result should be `Just x` for some value `x`.

Consider a simple example of summation of two `Maybe` values. Let's try to write an explicit version of such function:

```
SumExplicit.hs
```

Here we define an explicit type of function; this function takes two numbers of type `Num` class wrapped into the `Maybe` monad and returns their sum in case of success. As you can see, it is a quite lengthy and ugly definition of such sum. We have to duplicate the same case logic twice for each argument.

Let's take a look at how `Maybe` implements a monad type class in the `Prelude` list:

```
MaybePrelude.hs
```

If the value is `Just x` for some `x`, bind is defined as `f` applied to `x`. If the value is `Nothing`, then nothing can be passed on to `f`, and hence `Nothing` is returned. This means that once a function in a chain of monadic `Maybe` operations returns `Nothing`, the whole chain will return `Nothing`. The `Just` data constructor is a return operation. So let's rewrite summation using bind and return operations:

```
SumMonad.hs
```

It becomes more cryptic, but it is definitely a shorter version of the same function. To avoid such secret messages, Haskell has a `do` syntactic sugar for monads:

```
SumClear.hs
```

Now it is significantly better. The rule of thumb is that you should remember that implicit bind operations are inserted between lines.

The IO monad

Being a pure functional language, Haskell requires a marker of impure functions and IO monad is that marker. The `Main` function is an entry point for any Haskell program. It cannot be a pure function because it changes state of the "World", at least by creating a new process in OS. Let us take a look at its type:

```
Main.hs
```

The `IO ()` type signifies that there is a computation that performs an I/O operation and returns an empty result. There is really only one way to perform I/O in Haskell: Use it in the `main` procedure of your program. GHCi allows direct execution of any I/O code. It does so only because all the execution is already carried inside the IO monad of GHCi. Also it is not possible to execute an I/O action from an arbitrary function, unless that function is in the IO monad and called from `main`, directly or indirectly. Since IO is a monad that doesn't provide a way to extract a "real-world" component, once you get into the IO monad, you will be stuck with it. A pure function can be and will be always called from the I/O monad as program without inputs and outputs doesn't make any sense. But a pure function cannot call impure code. The do notation is used in the `main` function, just as it is used for any other monad.

I/O functions for standard input/output device are always useful:

```
StdIO.hs
```

You can use `putStr`/`putStrLn` to output a string to the standard output and `getLine` to read a line from the standard input.

Summary

In this chapter, we learned a bit of Haskell history, made a quick overview of language basics, and figured out how to install the Haskell platform. In the next chapter, we will continue getting into more advanced Haskell features, such as template Haskell and quasiquotes, along with building a tick database from CSV sources.

2
Getting your Hands Dirty

Market microstructure studies usually means messing a lot of data. One day of trade can easily generate more than 50 thousands of records for single liquid security. And we usually want a lot of securities and a lot of days, so security history databases might grow to enormous sizes. Therefore, we are going to explore three main stages of data preparation: data acquisition, data description, and data quality assessment.

Data acquisition is about getting raw data from exchange, ECN or ATS and putting them into a less common format. You might get inputs in a variety of data formats. **Comma Separated Values (CSV)**, XML, FIX – just to name a few of them. So the first step is to parse data and load them into a database in a format closely resembling the source.

Data description is a data enrichment process. Raw ticks from the previous stage get their descriptive values, for example, each tick can be marked after it happens at its opening or closing hours, day of the week, or if there was some significant news that day. Such data enrichment helps a lot to fetch the required data if a specific influence of events or circumstances are studied.

The domain model

These are the following main types of markets which exist:

- Order-driven
- Quote-driven

They differ in the way they quote and what kind of information is usually available from them. The common examples of order-driven markets are classical stock markets, such as **London Stock Exchange** (**LSE**) or **New York Stock Exchange** (**NYSE**). Those stock markets usually publish information about all trades that happened during the day and if you're listed on the exchange then order stream is also available. Quote-driven markets are usually Over-The-Counter markets; that is, when a broker provides a stream of buy and sell prices, completed trades, and sometimes active limit orders. Thus, in fact we have three base entities in our domain model: trades, orders, and quotes. All of them are found in their first approximation in `Domain.hs`.

Here we can see a record syntax of datatype declaration. By Haskell specification, for instance, `tTime` getter is a function of the `Trade -> LocalTime` type, that is, it takes a trade and extracts time field from it. There are no setters in Haskell because of data object immutability.

We don't mention security ticker or code in those datatypes because it is usually advisable to partition data by ticker from scalability and performance point of view.

The Attoparsec library

A CSV file is the most portable and widely used format for data transfer. In fact almost every data provider can provide CSV files. So we should be able to parse them in a fast and a type-safe manner.

Attoparsec is an amazing parser library written by *Brian O'Sullivan*. It is loosely based on the standard library `Parsec` but allows parsing of binary formats and also is useful for FIX parsers. It is written with performance and efficiency in mind.

To install the library you should use the packaging tool Cabal. For the first-time usage, Cabal should build index of packages available at the Haskell package repository Hackage (`http://hackage.haskell.org`) and then you should run an update process as follows:

```
cabal update
```

It might take some time depending on your network connectivity. It is advisable to make updates from time to time. After the update you should install the Attoparsec library by running the Cabal's install command:

```
cabal install attoparsec
```

Cabal will download all dependencies, build them, and finally compile and install the Attoparsec library.

Parsing plain text files

Consider parsing of a CSV file with quotes that can be obtained from a broker in the following format:

```
Time,Ask,Bid,AskVolume,BidVolume

01.10.2012 00:00:00.741,1.28082,1.28077,1500000.00,1500000.00
```

And our task is to parse such a file into data objects for further processing. A bit longer source code listing is found in `CsvParser.hs`, but we are going to walk through it and discuss every detail.

In the first line we define the `OverloadedStrings` language extension in a language pragma. The built-in `String` type is defined in Haskell as `type String = [Char]`. This may be inefficient in some contexts and we need to use more suitable string representation that could be, for instance, easier to manipulate, better performing or consuming less memory. This language extension instructs the compiler that strings in code could be of custom type and refer to our own representation. When enabled, strings no longer get the `String` type, but `IsString a => a`, where `IsString` is defined in `IsString.hs`.

There are a lot of `IsString` instances available for different types. In particular, the `Text` type, an efficiently packed String type, also have instance implementation. And, we are going to use this type extensively in parsing.

Next we declare the `CsvParser` module that exports two functions `csvFile` and `quote`, and the `Quote` datatype with all internals as two dots in brackets specify it. Then the bunch of imports of required modules goes. For the sake of simplicity, we have included the `Quote` type into this module.

Now the parser part starts defining the `csvFile` function. This function defines `Parser [Quotes]`. The `many1`Parser combinator applies the `quote` parser one or more times and returns a list of parsing results. Then the `endOfInput` parser matches only if all the input has been consumed. Idiomatically, one might read it as there are many quotes in input and then at the end of the input, parse strings to quotes and put them to the list. The `quote` parser is read in the same manner as the `csvFile` parser. It expects time and four doubles separated by commas and then ends the line and constructs the `Quote` object.

The `qcomma` parser uses the built-in `char` parser to match comma and discards the result of parsing. Also the Attoparsec library provides string parsers, `string` and `stringCI` (for case-insensitive match).

Of course, we can write our own time parser, but it is a bit more difficult and there already exists a library function, `parseTime` in the `Data.Time` module that can parse the time. Therefore, we take all letters till the comma is found, and then unpack the `Text` string into string and parse it using `parseTime`.

Parsing files in applicative style

To describe the applicative style, first we need to understand functors, or instances of the `Functor` type class. Typically, they are the structures that can be mapped over. The `Functor` type class defined in `Functor.hs`.

Thus `fmap` defines how to map a function to another function defined on the instances of this type class. It is illustrated with the `Maybe` functor in `MaybeFunctor.hs`.

Here we defined that if `Maybe` has a value, then the function must be applied to that value, otherwise `Nothing` should be returned. Thus we can promote a function over primitive types to another function between the two `Maybe` values.

Applicative functor is a functor with additional property: you can apply function inside a functor to values that can be either outside or inside the functor. This is defined in `Applicative.hs`.

So this definition introduces a class constraint. It says that each instance of the `Applicative` type class must also be an instance of `Functor`. Thus it has the `fmap` function for "outside" mapping. The `pure` function provides a method to inject value into the functor, or in other words it wraps a value into some default context. The `<*>` function has a type closely resembling the `fmap` type but it takes a functor with a function inside and applies it to the next functor and that is the `fmap` function for "inside". The real power of applicative functors lies in the ability to combine different computations such as I/O computations, non-deterministic computations, and so on.

The parser is rewritten in applicative style in `CsvParserApplicative.hs`.

What do we see here? The `Control.Applicative` import is added to support applicative functors. The `csvFile` function has become a one-liner. The `<*` operator has the `Applicative f => f a -> f b -> f a` type and it combines two actions discarding the value of the second operator.

The `quote` parser also shrunk to a few words. It uses the `<$>` operator that is defined in the `Data.Functor` module as `Functor f => (a -> b) -> f a -> f b` and it provides a convenient way to apply a function over an applicative functor. Please, also note that data constructor is also a function in Haskell and that is why we can combine a constructor and data with this operator.

The `qcomma` parser also became a one-liner. The `qtime` function has been restructured but it did not become simpler as it relies mainly on the time parsing function, rather than on Attoparsec. So the type-safe parser is just 15 lines long.

Outlier detection

Market data are not always clean, and in most cases one should verify the correctness and validity of the data. Though many obvious checks (such as positive price) can be easily implemented, some advanced algorithm should be used to identify an outlier. For our purposes, outlier is a price that appears to deviate significantly from other prices. It might be quite hard to quantify what "significant deviation" means. Here we take the simplest of statistical approaches and assume that prices are normally distributed, though it is not a correct assumption. Under this assumption it is possible to establish a quite simple test based on mean and standard deviation.

Essential mathematical packages

Though the basics of mathematics and statistics are easy to implement, in most cases, it is better to put this work off to already implemented and tested packages rather than manually reimplement all the required algorithms. Any algorithm requires data structures and functions over them. And the best implementation requires faster data structures and parallelizable algorithms. The package vector by *Roman Leshchinskiy* provides fast and efficient implementation of arrays. The installation process is very simple:

```
cabal install vector
```

This will download and compile package's sources. Then you can import it using the following code:

```
import qualified Data.Vector as V
```

The library must be imported with the `qualified` keyword because the module has a lot of functions with the same names as in the standard `Prelude` list. And the `qualified` import allows to avoid naming clashes. If there is no alias, `V`, the whole module name `Data.Vector` should be specified before each function from this module. The alias, `V` helps to reduce such burden and thus we should only specify the alias instead of the whole module name. After the import you can try several different methods as follows to create arrays:

```
Prelude> import qualified Data.Vector as V

Prelude V> :set +t

Prelude V> let x = V.fromList [1,2,3]
```

```
Loading package array-0.4.0.0 ... linking ... done.
Loading package deepseq-1.3.0.0 ... linking ... done.
Loading package primitive-0.5.0.1 ... linking ... done.
Loading package vector-0.10.0.1 ... linking ... done.
x :: V.Vector Integer
Prelude V> x
fromList [1,2,3]
it :: V.Vector Integer
Prelude V> V.singleton 5
fromList [5]
it :: V.Vector Integer
Prelude V> V.replicate 3 5.0
fromList [5.0,5.0,5.0]
it :: V.Vector Double
```

After the first line `:set +t` GHCi starts printing type after the evaluation. It might be also useful to switch on timing and memory statistics by using the `+s` flag.

The `fromList` function is quite common constructing objects from lists. You may encounter it in many libraries. The `singleton` and `replicate` functions are similar to the ones for lists from `Prelude`. Also vector might be constructed by applying a function to the index of each element in the list. The following call generates a vector of 10 elements in which each one of them is its index in the fourth power:

```
Prelude V> V.generate 10 (^4)
fromList [0,1,16,81,256,625,1296,2401,4096,6561]
it :: V.Vector Int
```

If you are planning to use only primitive types such as `Bool`, `Int`, `Double`, and `Complex` or tuples of them, then unboxed arrays are preferred, as they don't have runtime overhead. They have the same interface as the previously mentioned arrays, though they are imported using the following code:

```
import qualified Data.Vector.Unboxed as U
```

For working with unboxed arrays we require to remember a few of their particularities. At first, they are strict, so if you evaluate one element of the vector, all its elements will also be forced to evaluate. They might be more memory efficient as they pack all values into the linear piece of memory as it is usual for C/C++, for example; whereas the standard (or boxed) implementation stores only pointer either to a data structure, or to function that evaluates to the value of the cell. Also, such structure of unboxed vectors implies that they exists only for types with fixed sizes, otherwise, it is hard and inefficient to implement dynamic indexing of the array.

The next package that is essential for statistical computations is the `statistics` package again by *Brian O'Sullivan*. Its installation goes the same way as usual:

```
cabal install statistics
```

It includes a lot of standard statistical functions for descriptive statistics such as mean, variance, and other moments, thus providing a solid foundation for developing further algorithms.

Grubb's test for outliers

Grubb's test is a statistical test that is used to detect outliers in a data set coming from a normally distributed population. The test detects one outlier at a time. When this outlier is detected, it is removed from data set and the test is iterated until no outliers are detected.

The two-sided version of test, that is, test if the most distant point, maximum, or minimum of the data set is an outlier, calculates the following statistics:

$$G = \frac{\max\limits_{i=1..N} |y_i - m|}{s}$$

Here m and s are sample mean and standard deviation respectively. The hypothesis of no outliers is rejected at significance level α if:

$$G > \frac{N-1}{\sqrt{N}} \sqrt{\frac{t^2}{N-2+t^2}}$$

Here t is the upper critical value of the t-distribution with $N-2$ degrees of freedom and a significance level, $\frac{\alpha}{2N}$. As we usually manipulate with more than 10 thousands records at once, we can simplify the test by noting that the upper critical value grows faster than N with N going to infinity. Therefore, the correct square root is close to one, and the test statistics is as follows:

$$G > \frac{N-1}{\sqrt{N}}$$

Market prices are usually approximated by log normal distribution. So to satisfy normality precondition of the test, the input data set of ticks must be transformed as follows:

$$y_i = log\frac{x_{i+1}}{x_i} = logx_{i+1} - logx_i$$

Or otherwise in Haskell in `Normalize.hs`.

Here if the sorting trades by time using `LocalTime` is of type `Ord` class, then the sorted list of prices is fed to the `normalize` function that implements the whole logic. Note that we used a new syntactic construction, a point to join two functions. This point represents the function composition. It is implemented as a normal operator in Haskell and it has type: `(.) :: (b -> c) -> (a -> b) -> a -> c`. Therefore, the `normalize` function takes all trades, then applies `sortedPrices`, and at the end applies `normalize`, thus creating a pipeline.

Now we are ready to implement Grubb's outlier detection mechanism. This mechanism is found in `Grubbs.hs`.

As Haskell doesn't have loops, the algorithm should be presented in terms of the `filter` and `map` functions. At first, we define in the `getGtuple` function how to calculate G-score for each point, then `map` over input to get tuples of value and its score, then `filter` out to the outlier only vector and finally we are looking for the one item with the highest score.

Though the previous function provides the outlier value, the target function should return both an outlier value and new vector of prices.

Template Haskell, quasiquotes, type families, and GADTs

Object-Relational Mapping (**ORM**) is quite commonly used in web and enterprise development. The goal of ORM is to lower SQL boilerplate code and to simplify accessing data from multiple/different databases. There are many ORMs already implemented in each virtual programming language. The basic functionality of ORM is to represent database tables as objects in the language of choice with corresponding **Create-Read-Update-Delete** (**CRUD**) methods.

ORM implementation usually requires some tricky machinery to make them user friendly. Haskell is not an exception. One of the most robust ORM requires all those extensions from the chapter title. We won't cover all of them, as they are not usually visible in the client code but only in Template Haskell and quasiquotes.

Template Haskell is a GHC extension that allows you to generate Haskell code at compile time; that means, it is Haskell that generates Haskell. Though we will use some features of Template Haskell, we are not going to cover this topic in detail. All that need to know about is how to call Template Haskell (`Th`) functions as given in:

```
Th.hs
models
```

A nice feature of `Th` is that it can inject additional files during compilation; that is, all `Th` functions are executed inside an IO monad. Here we can see that syntactic construction `$(persistWithFile models)` instructs the Template Haskell compiler to execute the `persistWithFile` method that reads file models and constructs a new Haskell source code in place of the call. There is an option for GHC and GHCi: `-ddump-splices` that shows all the generated code. It might be quite useful for debugging heavily "templated" code.

The quasiquotes are minor extensions of Haskell and they allow embedding of arbitrary content into Haskell sources. During compilation, that content is parsed and transformed into Haskell code by the quasiquoter function. This is an effective way to embed any language into Haskell and it is quite often used to embed some variants of HTML, CSS, or Javascript. Also it gives a nice way to build sophisticated and embedded domain-specific languages. The previous piece of code can be rewritten with quasiquotes as as given in `Quasi.hs`.

Here, we just replaced `persistWithFile` with the `persistLowerCase` quasiquoter and embedded the `models` file content. The key point we should understand is that both the techniques allow automation of code generation.

Persistent ORM framework

There are a number of various Haskell bindings to the database interface, though most of them operate in the world of RDBMS and don't cooperate properly with the language itself. This means that all parsing and type-safety enforcements are up to the developer's will. This approach is not mistake-proof and requires a lot of boilerplate code that is hard to write and to maintain.

The ORM framework Persistent takes a different approach and tries to maintain type-safety and declarative syntax as much as possible. Also Persistent has other nice features. For instance, it easily adopts such NoSQL data stores such as MongoDB and CouchDB, because it is not focused on relational data models, and it makes the database framework agnostic.

Declaring entities

To start with any ORM framework we need to understand how to declare entities and how they are mapped to database structures. Let's recall our quote definition and try to map it in Persistent in `Quote.hs`.

You can see that we use the `persist` quasiquoter to define entities using Persistent's embedded language. Its output is a list of entity definitions. The `mkPersist` function takes this list and declares one datatype for each entity and an instance of the `PersistentEntity` type class that roughly corresponds to the database table. If we run GHCi with the `-ddump-splices` option, it prints out generated code, the essence of it is given in `QuoteOutput.hs`.

The framework assigns key field automatically, though for other type of database this key field would be defined differently. Also it translates those fields into corresponding Haskell fields and generates instance implementation. We will need a more sophisticated version of quote definition, which is present in `Quote2.hs`.

The `share` function will apply a list of functions to the same entity definitions. It will at first save definitions under the name `quoteDef`, and then create persistent definitions as in the previous example and finally make a migration function with name `migrateAll`. This migration function examines the current state of database, figures out differences in the model and the tables, and tries to apply changes; thus the database corresponds to model. The Persistent framework follows quite rigid rules for migrations and refuses to migrate if there is no safe way to do that. So you might quite rely on it.

Inserting and updating data

After we define the `Quote` entity, we should be able to create a new one using the code in `InsertUpdate.hs`.

So, here we run migration to ensure that our in-memory `sqlite` database has a table. In that table, we will insert one quote and update it after insertion. Let's try to compile and run it to see the following output:

```
$ ghc InsertUpdate.hs
[1 of 2] Compiling Quote2           ( Quote2.hs, Quote2.o )
Loading package ghc-prim ... linking ... done.
Loading package integer-gmp ... linking ... done.
Loading package base ... linking ... done.
..............
```

```
Loading package persistent-1.1.3.2 ... linking ... done.
Loading package persistent-template-1.1.2.1 ... linking ... done.
[2 of 2] Compiling Main             ( InsertUpdate.hs, InsertUpdate.o )
Linking InsertUpdate ...

$ ./InsertUpdate
2013-01-04 15:12:45.308818 UTC
Migrating: CREATE TABLE "Quote"("id" INTEGER PRIMARY KEY,"time" TIMESTAMP
NOT NULL,"ask" REAL NOT NULL,"bid" REAL NOT NULL,"askVolume" REAL NOT
NULL,"bidVolume" REAL NOT NULL)
Key {unKey = PersistInt64 1}
Quote {quoteTime = 2013-01-06 15:12:45.308818 UTC, quoteAsk = 1.2345,
quoteBid = 1.2355, quoteAskVolume = 100.0, quoteBidVolume = 230.0}
"End of program"
```

During the compilation phase you'll see a long list of modules as Persistent depends on a large set of Haskell modules and finally GHC produces a binary. When we run the binary, it prints out the time. Then the `migrateAll` function prints which SQL commands it issues to the database. In our case it creates the `Quote` table.

Then we come to the `insert` command. We just create a plain `Quote` object and give it to insert a function that returns a `QuoteId` object. This is a quite interesting and a differentiating point of Persistent: object and its identifier are separate entities. In most of the object-oriented and/or imperative languages, it is nearly impossible to remove the ID from an object, but in Haskell, the type system not only allows to separate, but also to enforce the `Quote-QuoteId` correspondence, that is, it is not possible to get anything but `QuoteId` in `Quote` inserts and vice versa for selects and updates.

The `update` function takes `QuoteId` and a list of updates to be applied on the entity. Apart from the assign operator, Persistent also has the following operators:

- Add (`+.`)
- Subtract (`-.`)
- Multiply (`*.`)
- Divide (`/.`)

Please note that, these update operators have a period at the end.

Fetching data

As we've got some data in the database we should now learn how to fetch it. The simplest query is to get the data by ID. Since the value might not exist in the database, it will return an object wrapped in `Maybe` using the following code:

```
quote <- get quoteId
```

The next possibility is to use `selectList`. It takes the following arguments:

- A list of filters
- A list of `SelectOps`

Let's start with filters and see how it works. These filters are found in `SelectList.hs`.

So far we have selected all quotes having bid price in the range from 1.0 up to 1.2 inclusively. Thus comma separator in the list means an `AND` operation. But also, we need an `OR` operation which is slightly more complicated as given in `SelectOr.hs`.

The disjunction represented by `||.` operator, that is, with a period at the end. And this means that we need both quotes with bid price from 1.0 up to 1.2 or with ask price from 0.8 up to 0.9.

There are four types of `SelectOps` defined in Persistent: `Asc`, `Desc`, `LimitTo` and `OffsetBy`, which is found in the `SelectOps.hs` file.

`Asc QuoteTime` sorts the output by using the time field in ascending order. `LimitTo 1000` limits the output to a thousand objects. And finally `OffsetBy 500` skips the first 500 objects.

Summary

In this chapter we have gone through the entire process of acquiring data, from getting the plain files up to loading the data. Using Attoparsec with `BinaryString` might help to us build a library to parse an FIX message, one of the heavily used financial protocol. Also we are prepared to further manipulate with data by introducing a persistent ORM library.

Thus we are able to build our own tick database either by free sources such as Yahoo! Finance, or by paid resource such as Reuters or Bloomberg. In the next chapter, we are going to use this data to build the first model of tick arrivals and try to calibrate the model against the real-word data.

3

Measuring Tick Intervals

In the previous chapter we have built a tick database. So we can start crunching our data to find some regularities and irregularities. This chapter contains much more math than previous as the topic becomes more analytical than the programmers' one. Market microstructure research usually goes into measurement of bid/ask price movements, spreads, volumes, and time intervals in between trades. Here we start with the simplest form of point processes applied to time intervals. But first, let us introduce main definitions that we are going to use throughout this chapter.

Point process

Let t denote time and let the random sequence $t_{i\in 1,2,\ldots}$ of increasing event arrival times $0 \le t_i \le t_{i+1}$ be called a point process on the line. We restrict ourselves to point processes on a timeline only. Moreover, we will consider only simple point processes, that is, without simultaneous occurrence of events, which effectively means that for all $it_i < t_{i+1}$ is true. In simple words, a point process is just a sequence of events marked by time of happening.

Counting process

If you try to count the number of events that happened in a point process from the start of the observation, you get a counting process. The strict definition is the process $N(t)$ with $N(t) = \sum_i I_{t_i \le t}$ is called a right continuous counting process associated with $\{t_i\}$, where I is a counting function. Thus, $N(t)$ is a right continuous step function with upward jumps at t_i of magnitude one. Moreover, the process $M(t)$ with $M(t) = \sum_i I_{t_i < t}$ is called a left continuous counting process and it counts the number of events that occurred before t.

Durations

Let's define the duration process, x_i associated with $\{t_i\}$, as a sequence of waiting times between two successive points, defined as follows:

$$x_i = \begin{cases} t_i - t_{i-1,} i = 2, \ldots, n \\ t_i, i = 1 \end{cases}$$

Furthermore, the $x(t)$ process with $x(t) = t - t_{M(t)}$ is called the backward recurrence time. It is a time elapsed from the previous point and is a left continuous function that grows linearly with discrete jumps back to zero after each arrival time.

Experimental durations

Before starting with further study of the counting process let us take a look at the experimental data of inter-tick durations and try to collect some statistical data based on empirical data.

As I had to use a legacy database table, appropriate mappings should be provided to Persistent for getting the right column names. Moreover, it is usually better to move entity definitions into a separate module. The definitions are usually reused in all the modules and separating them helps to avoid circular dependencies; otherwise, you might get the following error during compilation:

```
Module imports form a cycle:
         module `PullAndCollect' (PullAndCollect.hs)
        imports `CollectStats' (./CollectStats.hs)
  which imports `PullAndCollect' (PullAndCollect.hs)
```

This approach also helps to avoid Template Haskell requirement that the generated code should be put before the code it uses as in `LegacyTable.hs`.

In the legacy table description the `sql` option allows us to define a native SQL table and/or column to be use in generated SQL statements. There should be no whitespace between the equality sign and definitions; otherwise, quasiquoter will ignore the options and `EntityDefs` would be wrong. The ticks table has been stored in a MySQL database, so the Persistent initialization sequence will slightly differ as given in `PullAndCollect.hs`.

Here you can see that we use `runStderrLoggingT` to collect debugging information of the execution of SQL statement into the `stderr` output. For this case Persistent generates an obvious SQL equivalent of the query and prints the following output:

```
[Debug#SQL] "SELECT `id`,`dt`,`tt`,`ms`,`Ask`,`Bid`,`AskVolume`,`BidVolu
me` FROM `ticks_tmp` WHERE (`dt`=?) ORDER BY `tt`,`ms`"
```

The logic of statistics collection is in another module, `CollectStat`, and is a pure function over tick's list as it is usually better to split to pure and impure code. The function reuses the `statistics` library mentioned in the previous chapter in `CollectStats.hs`

Here we fixed the `histogram` function slightly to accept stricter intervals of bins. There is also a bunch of boilerplate functions such as daytime conversion and zipping. At the end, we are getting a CSV output that can be visualized in any plotting software. For instance, on a Mac one can use a built-in `Grapher.app` or an open source gnuplot (`http://gnuplot.org`).

The following graph is an example of the output of the program for EUR/USD pair for one trading day. It is in a logarithmic scale on the ordinate. We can see that the waiting time distribution quite loosely resembles the exponential one. If the model is precise, then the distribution should be a straight line, though, we see that times in range 0-2 seconds occur more often. Therefore, we should look for more general class of distributions to fit the model.

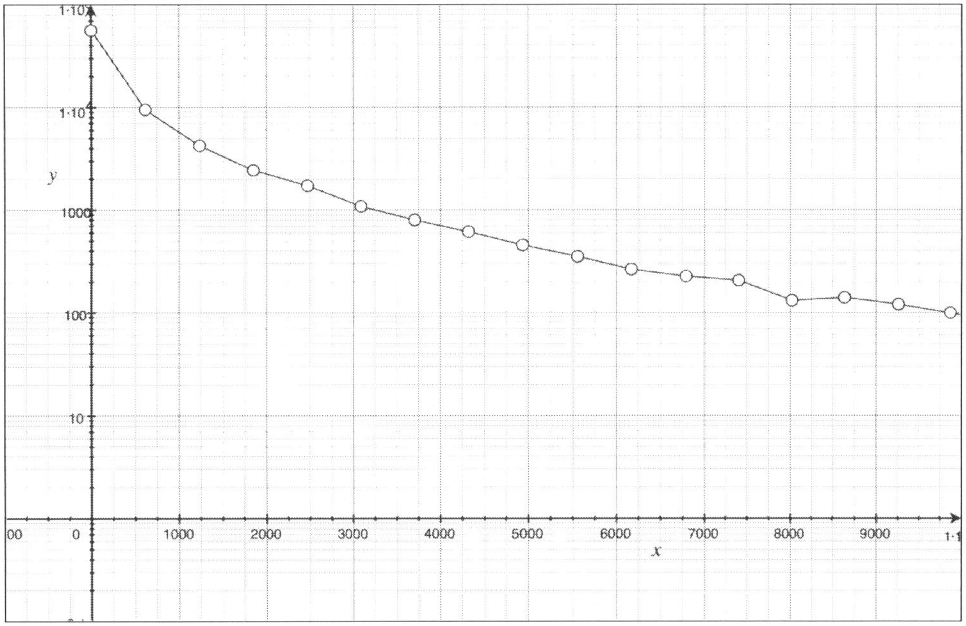

Lin-log histogram plot of inter-tick durations

Maximum likelihood estimation

Maximum likelihood estimation (**MLE**) is a statistical method of estimating the parameters of a statistical model. The essence of the method is to select a set of values of the model parameters that maximizes the likelihood function. Or in other words, this maximizes the probability that the data are described by that model with such parameter values.

To use the MLE method we should specify the joint density function for all observations from the data set. In the simple case of an independent and identically distributed sample, this function is as follows:

$$f\left(x_1, x_2, \ldots, x_n \mid \theta\right) = f\left(x_1 \mid \theta\right) \times f\left(x_2 \mid \theta\right) \times \ldots \times f\left(x_n \mid \theta\right)$$

Now let us look at this from a different perspective. Consider that the observed data are fixed parameters, whereas θ will be the function's variable and is allowed to vary freely; this function will be called the likelihood:

$$L\left(\theta \mid x_1, x_2, \ldots, x_n\right) = f\left(x_1, x_2, \ldots, x_n \mid \theta\right) = \prod_{i=1}^{n} f\left(x_i \mid \theta\right)$$

In practice it is often convenient to work with the logarithm of the likelihood function, called the log-likelihood, which is as follows:

$$L\left(\theta \mid x_1, x_2, \ldots, x_n\right) = \sum_{i=1}^{n} lnf\left(x_i \mid \theta\right)$$

Or as an average log-likelihood that might be more numerically stable:

$$\hat{l} = \frac{1}{n} L$$

The method of maximum likelihood estimates $L(\theta \mid x)$ by finding a value θ that is maximized:

$$\theta_{mle} = arg \max_{\theta \in o} L\left(\theta \mid x_1, x_2, \ldots, x_n\right)$$

One might also use log-likelihood or the average one, since the logarithm is a monotonically increasing function and therefore it doesn't affect the MLE estimate.

Generic MLE implementation

Such generic concepts implementation is the area where the Haskell support is brilliant. We consider one-dimensional observations. Let us start with the definition of the likelihood function in `Likelihood.hs`.

The likelihood function just maps the `theta` parameter and inputs a list of observations to the double value. The log-likelihood function is defined for this type class in a generic way, as it is defined in the previous chapter. It is not a good definition, and we need an additional constraint to make it better. Therefore, we introduce `IidPdf`, the probability density function of an independent and identically distributed sample. And that gives us an optimization opportunity and we can implement the instance of the class. But such flexibility requires two GHC extensions to be enabled, which are as follows:

- Flexible instances
- Undecidable instances

Finally we define a type class for a generic MLE estimation function assuming that the `argmax` function exists. The function is marked as `undefined` in the code. This is a universal definition of any function that breaks in runtime but provides a handy way to postpone implementation until the types are evolving and are not fixed. Though it is quite hard to define a generic version of the function, we will consider point processes with one parameter and then build a secant root finding algorithm.

Poisson process calibration

The simplest type of point processes is given by the Poisson process. It is a stochastic process that counts the number of events in a given time interval. The time between each pair of consecutive events has an exponential (Poisson) distribution and these inter-arrival times are mutually independent. The process is a good model of radioactive decay, it requests for a particular document on a web server, telephone calls, and many others. In the queuing theory job arrivals are usually assumed to be a Poisson process.

The following are the two principal conditions for counting the process as a Poisson process:

- Events don't occur simultaneously.
- Number of arrivals after t is independent of the previous number of arrivals (also called forgetfulness).

These two conditions in fact define the whole structure of the process. For example, they imply that the time between consecutive events are independent random variables.

First we start with the homogenous version of Poisson process, as it is one of the most well-known point processes. It is characterized by a rate parameter, λ (intensity), such that the number of events in the time interval, $(t, t+\tau)$ follows a Poisson distribution. The relation gives the following probability:

$$P\left[N(t+\tau)-N(t)=k\right]=\frac{(\lambda\tau)^k}{k!}e^{-\lambda\tau}$$

Here $N(t+\tau)-N(t)=k$ is the number of events in time interval, $(t, t+\tau)$. Whereas for one event per interval the formula is as follows:

$$P[\tau]=\lambda\tau e^{-\lambda\tau}$$

MLE estimation

If we have a set of tick intervals t_i let's try to infer the rate parameter of the Poisson process. According to the MLE procedure, the likelihood function should be constructed. The time intervals are independent of the process definition and probability of observing such time intervals is given as follows:

$$P_i=\lambda t_i e^{-\lambda t_i}$$

Therefore, we can write the following likelihood function as a joint probability density function:

$$L=\prod_{i=1}^{n}\lambda t_i e^{-\lambda t_i}=\lambda^n e^{-\lambda T}\prod_{i=1}^{n}t_i$$

Here $T=\sum_{i=1}^{n}t_i$ is the total time interval. That is the case where log-likelihood is better for analytic solution, and by using the logarithm it becomes:

$$logL=nlog\lambda-\lambda T+\sum_{i=1}^{n}log\,t_i$$

Now we should fix n and T and derivate by λ and equate it to zero:

$$\frac{\partial logL}{\partial \lambda} = \frac{n}{\lambda} - T = 0$$

Thus it yields to:

$$\lambda = \frac{n}{T}$$

And as we can see, the rate parameter now defines the number of events in a time unit.

Akaike information criterion

The **Akaike information criterion** (**AIC**) is a measure of goodness of fit of a statistical model. Being derived from the concept of information entropy, it provides a relative measure of information lost by model description in reality. The general definition of AIC is as follows:

$$AIC - 2k - 2logL$$

Here k is the number of model parameters and L is the maximized value of the likelihood function.

For the Poisson process the maximized log-likelihood value is as follows:

$$T - 1$$
$$log\, n - log$$
$$\frac{n}{T} - n = n$$
$$L = n\, log$$
$$log$$

As the process has only one parameter, AIC becomes:

$$T - 1$$
$$log\, n - log$$
$$AIC = 2 - 2n$$

Haskell implementation

Let's try to implement all the previous formulae in the microframework we've already started at the beginning of this chapter in `Poisson.hs`.

First, we add a definition of the `Aic` type class in terms of the `Likelihood` class. We define parameters as `Double` to avoid conversion because it is usually a constant value for the model. It should be moved to the `Likelihood` module though.

Then we introduce the `Poisson` type to keep the lambda value. Also we need a helper function, `sumAndLen`. Then we define all type classes: `Likelihood`, `IidPdf`, `MLE`, and `Aic`.

Renewal process calibration

One of the ways to generalize the Poisson process is to allow inter-arrival times to follow any probability distribution defined on a non-negative, real line. Such extension is called a renewal process. The inter-arrival time's independence and identical distribution are preserved.

In this chapter, we will go through the process with inter-arrival times drawn from the Levy distribution that has the following probability density function:

$$f(x;\mu,c)=\sqrt{\frac{c}{2\pi}}\frac{e^{\frac{-c}{2(x-\mu)}}}{(x-\mu)^{\frac{3}{2}}}$$

Here c is a scale parameter and μ is the location parameter. This is a special case of an inverse-gamma distribution and it is from stable distribution family that is quite often employed to describe fat-tailed data.

Levy distribution is defined on $[\mu;\infty]$. But trades can be placed as near as possible, therefore we assume that the location parameter is zero.

MLE estimation

In this case we will go directly with log-likelihood function, therefore, let's calculate the log probability density function:

$$log\, f(x;c)=\frac{1}{2}\left[log\, c-3\, log\, x-log\, 2\pi-\frac{c}{x}\right]$$

Though the constant parts of the equation are not significant for finding maximum, but due to Akaike information criterion we should keep them all. Now we can write down the log-likelihood function for the renewal process as follows:

$$logL = \frac{-1}{2} nlog2\pi + \frac{1}{2} nlogc - \frac{1}{2}\sum_{i=1}^{n}\left(3logt_i + \frac{c}{t_i}\right)$$

To find the maxima of the function we should calculate partial derivatives and equate them to zero:

$$\frac{\partial \log L}{\partial c} = \frac{n}{2c} - \frac{1}{2}\sum_{i=1}^{n}\left(\frac{1}{t_i}\right) = 0$$

And we can define the scale parameter as follows:

$$\frac{1}{c} = \frac{1}{n}\sum_{i=1}^{n}\frac{1}{t_i} = \frac{\tau}{n}$$

Here τ is a shortcut for the sum of inverse intervals. As you can see the scale parameter is a harmonic mean of observations.

The AIC for this type of process can be easily obtained by using the following formula:

$$AIC = 2 - n\,log\,2\pi + n\,log\frac{n}{\tau} - \sum_{i=1}^{n}\left(3\,logt_i + \frac{n}{\tau t_i}\right)$$

Cox process calibration

Cox process, also known as doubly stochastic Poisson process or mixed Poisson process, is a generalization of Poisson process where calculating the rate parameter is a stochastic process itself. To enforce positivity of the rate parameter we assume that it follows geometric Brownian process:

$$d\Lambda_t = \sigma\Lambda_t dW_t$$

Here, Λ_t is a rate process, σ is a rate process parameter, and dW_t is a Wiener process. The geometric Brownian motion is a model process for many "toy" models and it has quite simple formulas for calculating central moments:

$$E(\Lambda_t) = \Lambda_0$$

$$Var(\Lambda_t) = \Lambda_0\left(e^{\sigma^2 t} - 1\right)$$

The probability density of the rate process starting at x_0 is given by log normal distribution:

$$f(x,t,\sigma) = \frac{1}{x\sigma\sqrt{2\pi t}} e^{\frac{-(\iota n\frac{x}{x_0}+\frac{1}{2}t\sigma^2)^2}{z\sigma^2}}$$

This non-homogenous case is constructed by using the generalized rate function, as the expected number of events between time T_i and T_j as follows:

$$\lambda_{i,j} = \int_{T_i}^{T_j} \lambda(t)\,dt = \left(T_j - T_i\right)E\left[\lambda(t)\right]$$

Plugging in the stochastic process formula we obtained for $t_i \in \left[T_i, T_j\right]$:

$$\lambda_i = t_i E\left[\Lambda_t\right] = t_i \lambda_{i-1} = \lambda_0 \prod_{j=1}^{i} t_j = \lambda_0 \xi_i$$

As discussed previously, time intervals are inter-independent and the probability is described by the following formula:

$$P_i = \lambda_0 \xi_i e^{-\lambda_0 \xi_i}$$

MLE estimation

Now we are able to construct joint probability density:

$$L = \prod_{i=1}^{n} \lambda_0 \xi_i e^{\lambda_o \xi_i} = \lambda_0^n \prod_{i=1}^{n} \xi_i e^{-\lambda_o \xi_i}$$

We use the logarithm now to simplify the maximum likelihood function:

$$\lambda_0 \xi_i + \sum_{i=1}^{n} log \xi_i$$

$$logL = nlog\lambda_0 - \sum_{i=1}^{n}$$

Now fixing n and ξ_i we should calculate the derivative and assume it to be zero:

$$\frac{\partial \log L}{\partial \lambda_0} = \frac{n}{\lambda_0} - \sum_{i=1}^{n} \xi_i = 0$$

Thus the maximum likelihood estimate is as follows:

$$\lambda_0 = \frac{n}{\sum_{i=1}^{n} \xi_i}$$

Model selection

Now we have three models of tick intervals based on the Poisson process. But how should we choose the proper one? There are really a few so-called information criteria used in practice. They are **Bayesian Information Criterion** (**BIC**), likelihood ratio test, and Akaike information criterion. We will choose the last one for our use because it is relatively unrestricting on model assumptions and easy to follow in the context of an MLE procedure. For instance, the likelihood ratio test requires nested models, that is, you should use one general model and some specific case of the model to compare, and AIC doesn't have such a restriction. With BIC it is not that easy, but the following are the three main points for AIC:

- AIC is derived from principles of information

- BIC has a prior of $\frac{1}{N}$ (where N is the number of models in consideration) but our intuition says that the prior one also must depend on the number of free parameters to avoid overfit
- AIC is asymptotically optimal in case of regression if the "true" model is not in the given set of models

The rule for AIC model selection is simple - choose one with a minimal AIC. Let's denote those AIC values of models as $\{AIC_i\}$ and the minimal value as AIC_{min}. The $e^{AIC_{min}-AIC_i}$ value is the relative likelihood of model i, or alternatively the relative probability that the i th model minimizes the estimated information loss in `Aic.hs`.

The `bestModel` method uses a new function, `minimumBy` from the `Data.List` module that consumes a comparator function and a list of objects. And as the output we get a model and its corresponding AIC value.

The secant root-finding algorithm

All of the previous methods require a root finding function. We're going to implement a secant method for MLE purposes. This method is quite universal in the sense that it doesn't require anything more than a function. Other methods might require existence and analytic form of the first derivative or might put some restrictions on the function class. As most of the root finding methods, the secant method is a recurrent method, that is, the one which should repeat a step until some convergence criteria is met.

This recurrence relation defines the secant method:

$$x_n = x_{n-1} - f\left(x_{n-1}\right)\frac{x_{n-1} - x_{n-2}}{f\left(x_{n-1}\right) - f\left(x_{n-2}\right)}$$

As you can see the method requires two initial values x_0 and x_1 that should ideally lie close to the root. The implementation of this root finding method is pretty straightforward as in `Secant.hs`.

Here we define a data structure, `Secant` that might be either a converged version (`ConvergedSecant`) or an in-progress structure (`Secant`). At first, we define two utility methods, `isZero` and `invDerivative`. The `isZero` function tests if the value is close enough to zero. It is always good to remember that the `Double` type has problems with comparison as 1.999... and 2.0 are the same numbers essentially. The `invDerivative` function is an inverse of a finite difference version of function derivative.

Then we defined a `step` function that implements the functionality of the secant method. Please, notice the usage of the `ConvergedSecant` data constructor. It is used as a marker of a completed root finding process. Thus the main function, `root` is a quite simple recursive function that applies the `step` function until it converges. In fact, dividing in to two classes, converged and in-progress, specifies the exit condition in recursion of root finding.

The QuickCheck test framework

Haskell has a quite unique test framework that is ported to few other languages that support functional features such as ML, F#, and Scala. QuickCheck allows you to define a set of properties that must be held for the function to be valid. Then the framework generates a random data to test those properties. This technique is also named fuzzy testing.

The major restriction of the framework is that it can test only pure methods, that is, the one without any side effects. And this is quite reasonable because side effects can usually make irreproducible test cases. This restriction usually leads to complete separation of pure and I/O code. In fact, this separation helps a lot in automatic parallelization of computations because the compiler can reason about pure code and rearrange it to squeeze the maximum of CPU.

Let's see how QuickCheck can be used to verify correctness of mathematical code. We'll take our secant method for testing in `QuickTests.hs`.

In the first step we verify whether the value of the `isZero` function is in the neighborhood of zero. Therefore, we put the $|x| \leq \varepsilon$ test condition. Later in the `main` function we call `quickCheck` with `propZero` to verify it. Let's try for now to see how it works in the GHCi command prompt:

```
$ ghciQuickTests.hs
GHCi, version 7.4.2: http://www.haskell.org/ghc/  :? for help
Loading package ghc-prim ... linking ... done.
Loading package integer-gmp ... linking ... done.
Loading package base ... linking ... done.
[1 of 2] Compiling Secant           ( Secant.hs, interpreted )
[2 of 2] Compiling QuickTests       ( QuickTests.hs, interpreted )
Ok, modules loaded: QuickTests, Secant.
*QuickTests>quickCheckpropZero
Loading package array-0.4.0.0 ... linking ... done.
Loading package deepseq-1.3.0.0 ... linking ... done.
```

```
Loading package old-locale-1.0.0.4 ... linking ... done.
Loading package time-1.4 ... linking ... done.
Loading package random-1.0.1.1 ... linking ... done.
Loading package containers-0.4.2.1 ... linking ... done.
Loading package pretty-1.1.1.0 ... linking ... done.
Loading package template-haskell ... linking ... done.
Loading package QuickCheck-2.5.1.1 ... linking ... done.
+++ OK, passed 100 tests.
```

As we can see it passes the tests and `QuickCheck` reports that it has generated a hundred of test inputs to verify the property.

Then we define two simple mathematical functions, linear and square. These are used in tests of inverse derivative and the secant method itself. For `invDerivative` we check if it calculates properly the first derivative of linear function. The `==>` operator provides a convenient way to construct implications on generated inputs. The left side should resolve to `True` for inputs to be accepted for property testing. The function of numerical derivation must get two different points and that is the condition of the property. The two next properties `propLinearSolve` and `propSquareSolve` test root-finding algorithm on well-known functions. Let's try to run it and see if the implementation is correct:

```
*QuickTests> main
+++ OK, passed 100 tests.
+++ OK, passed 100 tests.
+++ OK, passed 100 tests.
(0 tests; 10 discarded)
```

The last test seems to be hanging. There is definitely something wrong with the current implementation of the secant method. We see that QuickCheck has discarded 10 inputs and none of the tests have been completed. Therefore, it hangs in the secant method. One might recall that the square function might have 0, 1, or 2 roots on real line. If you break the execution of the test by pressing *Ctrl* + *C*, you will see the inputs of currently running test:

```
^C*** Failed! Exception: 'user interrupt' (after 1 test):
-0.4822295608868578
1.8680344475488024
-2.61509940637565
0.6592565080155612
```

And we see that $a < 0$ and $b > 0$ and the equation $ax^2 - b = 0$ don't have a solution on real line. The secant method doesn't detect such condition and it might be a further improvement in the method itself. But now we will only pose a restriction, $a > 0$. After this fix, it is a bit better, though it is still hanging sometimes, as seen in the following output:

```
*QuickTests> main
+++ OK, passed 100 tests.
+++ OK, passed 100 tests.
+++ OK, passed 100 tests.
^C*** Failed! Exception: 'user interrupt' (after 63 tests):
25.102056112736896
156.69814915695184
165.40429713832876
-2403.0767634065437
```

Now the reason seems to be an incorrect choice of starting points. We might improve it by putting one point to zero and the other $0 < x \le \frac{b}{a}$. Now the final code looks similar to the one in `QuickTests2.hs`.

The result of this work is still not good enough:

```
*QuickTests> main
*** Gave up! Passed only 18 tests.
```

It means that the conditions are too restrictive and it cannot effectively generate input data. There are test data modifiers to solve such problems.

QuickCheck test data modifiers

The framework comes with a bunch of predefined test modifiers such as `Positive` and `NonZero`. By using these modifiers the test code becomes more idiomatic. Take a look at the property in the `QuickTestsMod.hs` file.

The module imports `Test.QuickCheck.Modifiers` to access modifiers. The modifiers have pretty obvious names. Now the number of tests run is more than what it was previously but still it discards a lot:

```
*QuickTests2> main
*** Gave up! Passed only 72 tests.
```

Now one of the ways to handle such a situation is to increase the discard ration in the configuration of the `quickCheck` method:

```
*QuickTests2> let args = Args Nothing 100 100 100 True
*QuickTests2>quickCheckWithargspropSquareSolve
+++ OK, passed 100 tests.
```

Now it passes `OK`. The next question is code coverage. Does this cover a lot of original source code? Did we check all possible paths in the algorithm? Let's make a final test suiteas given in `QuickTestsFull.hs`.

Now we should compile it using **HPC** (**Haskell Program Coverage**) support:

```
$ ghc -fhpcQuickTestsFull.hs
```

Then run tests as normal executables:

```
$ ./QuickTestsFull
+++ OK, passed 100 tests.
+++ OK, passed 100 tests.
+++ OK, passed 100 tests.
+++ OK, passed 100 tests.
```

The trace of the program is written into the `.tix` files and into the `.mix` files in the `.hpc` directory. The `hpc` reporting tool uses these files. It is capable of generating text and HTML reports. The basic report is textual. It is usually a good idea to exclude `quickCheck` and test script from the report; therefore, we will use the `--exclude` flag:

```
$ hpc report QuickTestsFull --exclude=Main --exclude=QC
 97% expressions used (45/46)
 50% boolean coverage (1/2)
      50% guards (1/2), 1 always True
     100% 'if' conditions (0/0)
     100% qualifiers (0/0)
 80% alternatives used (4/5)
100% local declarations used (2/2)
100% top-level declarations used (4/4)
```

We see that the script tests consist of 100 percent of top-level and local declarations, though one guard condition has not been tested. The HTML report can help us to find this out as it contains a detailed, line-by-line report.

```
$ hpc markup QuickTestsFull --exclude=Main --exclude=QC
Writing: Secant.hs.html
Writing: hpc_index.html
Writing: hpc_index_fun.html
Writing: hpc_index_alt.html
Writing: hpc_index_exp.html
```

Now we can open `hpc_index.html`. By clicking on the name of the module **Secant** we can see its source with executed lines in bold and non-tested lines in yellow. Also it always shows true conditions in green.

Summary

In this chapter we came across mathematical and engineering tasks. We have learned a bit of point processes by means of a simple Poisson process. Maximum likelihood estimation is a powerful method for point process estimations.

On the engineering side we've started the implementation of generic MLE framework and come through possible pitfalls with a secant root-finding algorithm. Now we can employ the QuickCheck property-based testing to ensure that the mathematical code is correct under any condition. Also, a coverage tool is presented as a helper for finding non-tested spots in the source code.

In the next chapter, we will explore autoregressive models for counting processes. Quite usually model calibration and prediction should be nearly a real-time process, so we will take a look at GHC internals to use its optimizer properly.

4
Going Autoregressive

In this chapter we are going to introduce a model that is of the class of **Multiplicative Error Models** (**MEM**). It is a general class of time series models. A random variable is decomposed into the product of conditional mean and error term. Alternatively such models might be classified as **autoregressive conditional mean models** (**ACM**), where conditional mean follows a stochastic process with respect to filtration. In high frequency finance, Engle and Russel introduced an MEM to model behavior of inter-trade times and named it as **autoregressive conditional duration model** (**ACD**). The model itself is a special version of MEM applied to inter-trade durations.

Through the chapter we will start with a simple **Autoregressive-moving-average** model (**ARMA**) to see how **Maximum Likelihood Estimation** (**MLE**) works here and then extrapolate it to the ACD model.

The ARMA model definition

As we are working with positive-valued data, it is natural to convert them to log domain to enforce positive constraint. Thus, in further equations the restriction of positive price is removed. In log domain, traditional time series models can be easily applied. A simple autoregressive model ARMA(P,Q), where P refers the autoregressive terms and Q refers the moving average terms is given by the following equation:

$$x_i = \sum_{j-1}^{P} b_j x_{i-j} + \sum_{j-1}^{Q} c_j \varepsilon_{i-j} + \bar{\varepsilon}_i$$

In the preceding equation, ε is a white noise variable. A quite common assumption is that the noise is an independent, identically distributed random variable sampled from normal distribution with zero mean, though the direct maximum likelihood method could be applied to estimate parameters of this linear model. In my opinion the most elegant method is the Kalman filter. It is a recursive algorithm that consumes noisy input data to produce a statistically sound estimate of the system state.

The Kalman filter

The Kalman filter uses a system's model and multiple measurements over time to estimate the system's variables with less noise than what could be obtained from a single measurement. In fact each measurement might be seen as an estimate. The filter averages such estimates and comes up with a better system state.

The Kalman filter assumes that the system model is a linear stochastic model of the following form:

$$x_i = F_i x_{i-1} + B_i u_i + w_i$$

In the preceding equation, F is a state transition model applied to the previous state x_{i-1}, B is a control-input model applied to control vector u_i, and w_i is a white noise with covariance Q. As there is no control input for time series, the system model simplifies as follows:

$$x_i = F_i x_{i-1} + w_i$$

The next model required by filter is an observation model; that is an assumption on how noisy observations of true state are. This is shown by the following equation:

$$z_i = H_i x_{i-1} + v_i$$

In the preceding equation, H is an observation model and v is a zero mean Gaussian white noise with covariance R, which is represented as follows:

$$v_i \sim N\left(0, R_i\right)$$

The Kalman filter is a recursive filter; that is, a new measurement and estimated state is required to compute the current state. The filter's state consists of a state estimate x_i and an error covariance matrix P_i.

The filter has two steps:

- **Predict**: This step takes the estimated state from the previous time step and produces an estimate for the current time step. The predicted state is usually called a priori estimate.
- **Update**: In this step the predicted step is updated by the new observation to refine the estimated state and to produce a posteriori estimate.

In the predict phase, a priori estimates (with hat) are obtained by the following equations:

$$\hat{x}_i = F_i x_{i-1}$$

$$\hat{P}_i = F_i P_{i-1} F_i^T + Q_i$$

Thus, the Kalman filter makes two assertions. First, the system state evolves as if there is no noise. Second, the system and measurement noises are incorporated into the error covariance matrix. Then a new measurement arrives and the filter's state should be updated by innovation y (measurement residual) and innovation covariance S:

$$y_i = z_i - H_i \hat{x}_i$$

$$S_i = H_i \hat{P}_i H_i^T + R_i$$

The update phase is quite dependent on what the close estimate means, but for common minimum mean square error the equations are as follows:

$$K_i = \hat{P}_i H_i^T S_i^{-1}$$

$$x_i = \hat{x}_i + K_i y_i$$

$$P_i = (I - K_i H_i) \hat{P}_i$$

In the preceding equation, K_i is an optimal Kalman gain and I is an identity matrix.

Matrix manipulation libraries in Haskell

For the Kalman filter, we would require the matrix manipulation library. At the time of writing there were a few libraries to choose from, which are as follows:

- **Matrix** (`http://hackage.haskell.org/package/matrix`): Matrix is a Haskell native implementation of basic matrix operations and few algorithms. It is in early development stage and not in production right now but it might be good for prototyping without a lot of dependencies.
- **Repa** (`http://hackage.haskell.org/package/repa`): The Repa library provides high performance, regular, multi-dimensional, and parallel arrays. The nice feature of Repa is that it automatically parallelizes all computations over arrays. Though the library targets mainly image processing, it misses some quite common algorithms such as matrix decompositions and matrix-vector multiplication.
- **Accelerate** (http://hackage.haskell.org/package/accelerate): Accelerate is a quite unique project that targets GPGPU computations. It is quite fascinating to be able to write the code that might be executed either on CPU or on GPU. Though it requires some shift in coding style, it might be worth doing it, if massive parallel computations are required. Currently it supports NVIDIA's CUDA, Opens and Repa backends.
- **HMatrix** (`http://hackage.haskell.org/package/hmatrix`): The HMatrix library provides access to open-source libraries such as **GNU Scientific Library** (**GSL**), **Basic Linear Algebra Subprograms** (**BLAS**), and **Linear Algebra Package** (**LAPACK**). It has some issues with compilation of those libraries under Windows but there is some work around for making it work. However, under Linux and Mac OS, its installation is quite smooth. The library provides quite reasonable performance and usability. Also there exist a few spin-offs that provide interoperability with Repa and GSL Statistics.

HMatrix basics

The basic matrix is represented by the `Data.Packed.Matrix` datatype, though vector is a special case of matrix, it is represented by a different datatype, `Data.Packed.Vector`. Both datatypes implement `Num`, `Fractional`, and `Floating` type classes. Therefore they support such common operations as addition, multiplication, and so on. But you should be careful as they are element-wise operations. Let's take a look at the example in `MatrixBasics.hs`.

In this example we collected the most common matrix operations. First, we created two 2 x 2 matrices using the `><` operator that takes dimensions and list of values as shown in the following example:

```
(><) :: Int -> Int -> [a] -> Matrix a
```

Matrices and vectors support the standard classes `Show` and `Read`, so it is quite easy to print them out. As floating-point operations often yield ugly numbers, the `disp` function might be used to print out matrices in rounded format. Try to run the script and the output should be as follows:

```
"Matrix A"
(2><2)
 [  1.0, 2.0
 , -2.0, 1.0 ]
"Matrix B"
(2><2)
 [ 0.0, 1.0
 , 1.0, 0.0 ]
```

Also it is possible to add and multiply matrices. Note the difference between the element-wise star (`*`) operator and the classic matrix multiplication operator `<>`.

```
"A + B"
(2><2)
 [  1.0, 3.0
 , -1.0, 1.0 ]
"A x B"
(2><2)
 [ 2.0,  1.0
 , 1.0, -2.0 ]
"A * B"
(2><2)
 [  0.0, 2.0
 , -2.0, 0.0 ]
"B x A"
(2><2)
 [ -2.0, 1.0
 ,  1.0, 2.0 ]
```

The library not only provides primitive operations but also some more complicated ones like least-squares solver based on singular value decomposition. The output in our examples should be as follows:

```
"A \\ B"
(2><2)
 [ -0.3999999999999999, 0.19999999999999996
 ,  0.2000000000000001, 0.39999999999999997 ]
2x2
-0.40  0.20
 0.20  0.40

"Check A x C = B"
2x2
0.00  1.00
1.00  0.00
```

The Kalman filter in Haskell

As described earlier in the chapter, the Kalman filter has the following independent parts:

- System model (we will remove control-input model from system model as we cannot control the market)
- Observation model
- Kalman gain

It would be quite logical to split the filter into such parts. Let's try to model it in `KalmanFilter.hs`.

First, we need to specify a system model that includes transition matrix and noise covariance. This is represented by `SystemModel` datatype. Quite similarly the observation model is defined. Those two models are combined into a single type system that specifies the whole model.

Then, we introduce system state and system observations as `newtype` declarations. They are essentially the same as vector double type though introduction of different types ensures that they won't be mixed somewhere in client code.

Finally, we define the Kalman filter's state and two functions: `predict` and `update` that implement the filter's algorithm. Now we are going to combine them into a single processing function that takes a stream of observations as input and modifies filter state accordingly, as in `KalmanChain.hs`.

This function definition might be rewritten in eta reduction style. Technically speaking, eta reduction is a dropping of abstraction over a function, or simply dropping parameters of function. For example, `\x -> abs x` is reduced to `abs` under eta conversion. In `estimate` function, we can easily drop kalman and observations. And in `singlestep` function only `obs` is dropped as shown in `KalmanEta.hs`.

Eta reductions quite often lead to the so called point-free programming style. It is quite natural for a functional programmer to think about programs in terms of function composition without mentioning actual parameters. Moreover, Haskell supports such style by providing the dot operator. Thus two definitions below are equivalent in `Zeta.hs`.

The latter expression is clearer and more high level as it describes functions as composition, and not as a sequential application. Though point-free style extensively uses points in function composition, the term came from topology, the branch of mathematics studying spaces with points and functions over those spaces. And point-free function definition doesn't mention the point of space it acts upon. In Haskell, that space is type and points are values of those types. But abuse of point-free style might lead to obfuscation and pointless style. So be careful.

The state-space model for ARMA

Now going back to math to combine both pieces into single estimation techniques, the Kalman filter operates over the state and requires a model of system dynamics. Essentially this state is a vector that totally specifies the system behavior at a given time.

Let's downscale our discussion to the ARMA(1,1) model to simplify the whole thing; the model as follows:

$$x_i = bx_{i-1} + c\varepsilon_{i-1} + \overline{\varepsilon_i}$$

With a naive approach we can rewrite it in matrix form as follows:

$$X_i = FX_{i-1} + w_i = \begin{pmatrix} b & 1 \\ 0 & 0 \end{pmatrix} \begin{pmatrix} x_{i-1} \\ 0 \end{pmatrix} + w_i \begin{pmatrix} 1 \\ c \end{pmatrix}$$

The observation model just picks the first element of the vector in this case without observation noise as shown in the following equation:

$$Z_i = H_i X_i = \begin{pmatrix} 1 & 0 \end{pmatrix} \begin{pmatrix} x_i \\ 0 \end{pmatrix}$$

Now given the model estimated we can forecast the future values of both time series and error term.

ARMA in Haskell

It is not hard to represent the ARMA model in Haskell, though it would be great to make an extension point, so we could potentially give any model to the Kalman filter. Thus, we can make a `ToSystem` type class that would be responsible for the conversion in `ToSystem.hs`.

Here we define three functions that convert from abstract model to system model specified previously for the Kalman filter. Also we make an instance for `System` type as well to avoid conversion costs in the following modification of the `predict` and `update` functions in `predict.hs`.

Let's use the prototype ARMA model from `Arma.hs`.

The implementation of `toSystemModel` and `toObservationModel` is quite trivial re-writing of previous state model equations.

ACD model extension

The basic idea of the autoregressive conditional duration model is to parameterize conditional mean function as follows:

$$\varphi_i = \varphi_i(\theta) = \mathrm{E}[x_i;\theta]$$

In the preceding equation, θ is a model parameter vector. Then it is assumed that the standardized durations $\varepsilon_i = \frac{x_i}{\varphi_i}$ follow an **independent and identically distributed (i.i.d)** process with $\mathrm{E}[\varepsilon_i] = 1$. Complete specification of ACD model requires either choice of conditional mean function form or choice of standardized durations distribution.

The basic ACD specification is a linear decomposition of the conditional mean function $\varphi_i = a + \sum_{j=1}^{P} b_j x_{i-j} + \sum_{j=1}^{Q} c_j \varphi_{i-j}$ with non-negativity sufficient conditions $a > 0$ and $b \geq 0, c \geq 0$. For the sake of simplicity we will consider a model with $P = 1, Q = 1$ and $\varphi_i = a + bx_{i-1} + c\varphi_{i-1}$.

For this model, the unconditional mean is easily computed as the mean of durations is 1.

$$\mathrm{E}[x_i] = \mathrm{E}[\varepsilon_i]\mathrm{E}[\varphi_i] = \mathrm{E}[\varphi_i]$$

Let's compute a mean of the model equation as follows:

$$\mathrm{E}[\varphi_i] = a + b\mathrm{E}[x_{i-1}] + c\mathrm{E}[\varphi_{i-1}]$$

Now assuming some stationary process and conditional mean; that is, $\mathrm{E}[x_i] = \mathrm{E}[x_{i-1}]$ and $\mathrm{E}[\varphi_i] = \mathrm{E}[\varphi_{i-1}]$, we obtain the equation for unconditional mean as follows:

$$\mathrm{E}[x_i] = a + b\mathrm{E}[x_i] + c\mathrm{E}[x_i]$$

And by solving it:

$$\mathrm{E}[x_i] = \frac{a}{1-b-c}$$

The unconditional variance computation is a bit more involved but derived in the same way as follows:

$$\mathrm{Var}[x_i] = \mathrm{E}[x_i]^2 \, \mathrm{Var}[\varepsilon_i] \frac{1 - c^2 - 2bc}{1 - (c+b)^2 - c^2 \mathrm{Var}[\varepsilon_i]}$$

The autocorrelation function is derived as follows:

$$\rho_1 = \mathrm{Cov}(x_i, x_{i-1}) = \frac{b(1 - c^2 - bc)}{1 - c^2 - 2bc}$$

$$\rho_n = (b + c)\rho_{n-1}$$

Covariance stationarity conditions are satisfied by the following function:

$$(b + c)^2 - b^2 \mathrm{Var}[\varepsilon_i] < 1$$

And it is quite similar to GARCH stationarity conditions.

Experimental conditional durations

Before starting with the model application, let us take a look at how those durations behave in time scale and how they depend on previous one. In fact we can consider few plots to estimate as follows:

- Autocorrelation function
- Lagged plots

Based on these two charts we will estimate and model a behavior of the durations.

The Autocorrelation function

The Autocorrelation function is often used in signal processing and is a correlation of time series against itself lagged by a few steps. Usually for discrete observations the estimate of autocorrelation function is obtained as follows:

$$R(k) = \frac{1}{n-k}\frac{1}{\sigma^2}\sum_{t=1}^{n-k}(x_t - \mu)(x_{t+k} - \mu)$$

In the preceding equation, k is a lag and is less than n, x_t is an observation at moment t; μ is the mean and σ^2 is the variance. The biasness of this estimate depends on how mean and variance are obtained. In an ideal case, it would be unbiased if mean and variance are true. In practical cases, it would be biased and it is just a matter of minimization of a mean square error.

The brute force algorithm of autocorrelation computation has complexity of n^2. Therefore, it is useful only in a limited number of cases. The statistics package provides such implementation, though optimized for stream fusion. It is an automatic optimization technique that removes intermediate data structures to lower the pressure on memory allocation and to produce a performant code. Also it motivates us to use a high-level coding style, thus avoiding tricky optimizing code manipulations that make your code unreadable.

The optimized version of autocorrelation algorithm uses Wiener-Khinchin theorem. It states that the autocorrelation function of a stationary random process has a spectral decomposition given by the power spectrum of that process. Thus we can use **Fast Fourier Transform** (**FFT**) to reduce complexity to $n \log n$. The algorithm itself has three steps:

$$F(t) = FFT(x_t)$$

$$S(f) = F(f)F^*(f) = |F(f)|$$

$$R(\tau) = IFFT[S(f)]$$

In the preceding equation, $IFFT$ is an inverse FFT and the asterisk is a complex conjugate in `Autoregression.hs`.

The statistics library provides both transformations. Though its main goal was a correct and provide easy to read implementation, it is not the most performant implementation of Fourier transform. If performance is the must, then it is better to re-use bindings to C-library FFTW. Also we can see that Haskell has a built-in support of complex numbers with parameterized inner type, but only `Double` and `Float` make sense to be used. Complex numbers have an unusual form of data constructor. Though it is completely fine from the language point of view and it is not an exception, the fact is that data constructors are just functions that return the new object. In GHCi we can test it as follows:

```
Prelude> import Data.Complex
Prelude Data.Complex> :t (:+)
(:+) :: a -> a -> Complex a
Prelude Data.Complex>
```

The `t` command allows inspection of types of any function or object. By type signature we can say that `:+` just takes two arguments of the same type `a` and returns `Complex a`.

Stream fusion

As we've already mentioned, stream fusion is the compiler optimizations technique that removes intermediate data structures to lower the pressure on memory allocation and to produce performant code. Also it motivates us to use a high-level coding style, thus avoiding tricky optimizing code manipulations that make your code unreadable.

Lists and arrays, or any other traversable data structure, can be represented as a continuous stream of values of the same type. Stream fusion framework provides two datatypes to cope with such representation.

```
data Stream a = forall s. Stream (s -> Step s a) s
```

The `forall` keyword allows us to bring a new type variable into scope. It is not needed in function definitions as it is assumed by default, but for datatype constructors it might be useful to hide internal types. This keyword is a part of GHC extension `ExistentialQuantification` and such datatypes are called existentially quantified types.

So, the stream consists of step function and initial seed. The step function produces a next element and a new state from the current state of stream as in `Stepper.hs`.

As we see at the definition of step, the results of the `step` function can be as follows:

- `Yield a s` contains an element and the next seed
- `Skip s` says that current step doesn't contain an element
- `Done` flags the end of a stream

It is relatively easy to write a straightforward conversion function from list to stream in `ListToStream.hs`.

In this example we used the list as initial seed and passed list tail further to keep the state of the stream. Though any data structure can be used as seed, it should be carefully selected to be lazy, thus avoiding both excessive optimizations (as it might run the same computation in parallel) and eager computation of the seed. Also the reverse function could be defined with type `streamToList :: Stream a -> [a]`.

In the next step all list and array operations can be expressed in terms of stream manipulation as follows:

```
func = streamToList . transformation . listToStream
```

For instance, the `filter` implementation uses `Skip` data constructor to mark nonmatched entries of the input list.

GHC also contains the rule that allows us to remove any occurrence of list construction followed by its consumption; that is, the following property is true for streams:

```
forall s. listToStream (streamToList s) = s
```

By stream fusion techinch GHC collects an individual operation over elements of traversable data structure into a single tight loop.

The Autocorrelation plot

And returning back to durations, we can see on the autocorrelation plot that there are significant nonzero autocorrelations on lagged durations. If they were random, autocorrelations would be near zero for any and all lagged durations. Therefore, we can conclude that there is some autocorrelated process of durations.

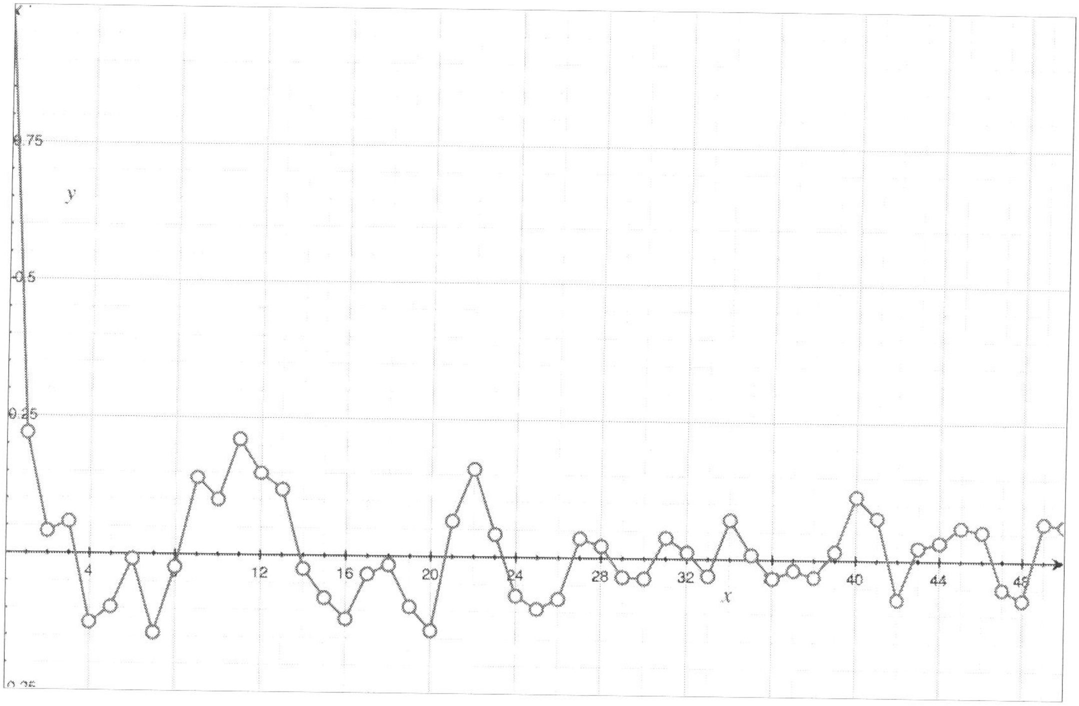

QML estimation

The exponential distribution is a quite natural choice for the distribution of intergrade durations. So we will take an exponential ACD (E-ACD) model as a starting point for studying this model class. Though this model might be a quite restrictive, it allows us to build a relatively simple framework for quasi-maximum likelihood estimations of ACD.

The likelihood contribution of a single observation is given by the following distribution:

$$f\left(x_i\right)=\frac{1}{\varphi_i}e^{-\frac{x_i}{\varphi_i}}$$

And log likelihood is given by the following equation:

$$l(x_i) = \log f(x_i) = -\frac{x_i}{\varphi_i} - \log \varphi_i$$

Therefore, if x_i are observations, then quasi-log likelihood function is as follows:

$$\log L = -\sum_{i=1}^{n} \frac{x_i}{\varphi_i} + \log \varphi_i$$

Assuming that $\varphi_i(\theta)$ is a function of parameters θ, the quasi-log likelihood has its extrema where partial derivatives are zero:

$$\frac{\partial L}{\partial \theta} = \sum_{i=1}^{n} \frac{\partial \varphi_i}{\partial \theta} \frac{1}{\varphi_i} \left[\frac{x_i}{\varphi_i} - 1 \right]$$

Let's try to simplify the expression under the sum sign by noticing the following:

$$\frac{\partial \varphi_i}{\partial \theta} \frac{1}{\varphi_i} = \frac{\partial \log \varphi_i}{\partial \theta} = \frac{\partial \log x_i}{\partial \theta} - \frac{\partial \log \varepsilon_i}{\partial \theta} = -\frac{1}{\varepsilon_i} \frac{\partial \varepsilon_i}{\partial \theta}$$

We can express partial derivative without the conditional mean function as follows:

$$\frac{\partial L}{\partial \theta} = \sum_{i=1}^{n} [1 - \varepsilon_i] \frac{1}{\varepsilon_i} \frac{\partial \varepsilon_i}{\partial \theta}$$

Now if standardized duration is drawn from exponential distribution with $\mathrm{E}[\varepsilon_i] = 1$, its distribution should look as follows:

$$f(\varepsilon) = e^{-\varepsilon}$$

Downloading the example code

You can download the example code files for all Packt books you have purchased from your account at `http://www.packtpub.com`. If you purchased this book elsewhere, you can visit `http://www.packtpub.com/support` and register to have the files e-mailed directly to you.

State-space model for ACD

ACD model might be represented as state space model as well. Let's reconsider the original model as follows:

$$\varphi_i = a + bx_{i-1} + c\varphi_{i-1}$$

$$\varphi_i = a + b\varphi_{i-1}\varepsilon_{i-1} + c\varphi_{i-1} = a + \left(b\varepsilon_{i-1} + c\right)\varphi_{i-1}$$

$$\begin{pmatrix} x_i \\ \varphi_i \\ 1 \end{pmatrix} = \begin{pmatrix} 1 & 0 & 0 \\ b & c & a \\ 0 & 0 & 1 \end{pmatrix} \begin{pmatrix} x_{i-1} \\ \varphi_{i-1} \\ 1 \end{pmatrix}$$

Summary

In this chapter we walked through the autoregressive models. The ARMA model has been revised in conjunction with the Kalman filter and its possibility to estimate hidden model state.

The autoregressive conditional duration model is a broad class of inter-tick time interval model. The further extensions are possible in formulation of probability.

On the technical side, we learned a set of matrix manipulation libraries in Haskell and took a closer look at HMatrix. We also looked at the stream fusion mechanism that has a great influence on the coding style in Haskell.

In the next chapter, we will learn another important financial concept—volatility. Also we will go through Haskell's approach to computation parallelization.

5
Volatility

Volatility is a specific measure of price variation of a financial instrument over time. There are two definitions of volatility that are used in finance. The most trivial one is a historic volatility that is usually calculated directly from past time series. An implied volatility is calculated from the observation of price of derivative instruments. Quite often option chain prices are used.

Historic volatility estimators

The standard definition of volatility is the square root of variance and it is usually defined as:

$$\sigma^2 = VarX = \frac{1}{N}\sum_{i=1}^{N}\left(x_i - \overline{x}\right)^2$$

Here x_i is the logarithmic return, $\overline{x}$ is the sample mean return, and N is the sample size. Volatility is usually expressed in annualized terms. For those purposes, it should be multiplied by the square root of trading periods in a year. If the daily volatility is calculated, then the coefficient $\sqrt{252}$ is used, because there are 252 trading days in a year.

Sample mean return is very hard to estimate because it is pretty noisy and it is quite unstable if the time interval changes. Therefore, the mean return is usually considered to be zero. Moreover, this trick has some theoretical grounds in risk-free measure pricing algorithms and it will be considered later in this book. Thus the volatility simplifies to:

$$\sigma^2 = \frac{1}{N}\sum_{i=1}^{N}x_i^2$$

This definition doesn't make any assumptions about price process distribution. Therefore, it is generally applicable. Variance in general has the following properties:

- **Non-negativity**: $VarX \geq 0$
- **Variance of constant**: $Var c = 0$
- **Scaling by constant**: $Var aX = a^2 Var X$
- **Sum of random**: $Var\left[aX + bY\right] = a^2 Var X + b^2 Var X + 2abCov\left(X, Y\right)$

This is what we should know about volatility basics.

Volatility estimator framework

So, let's define the estimation task in terms of type classes and datatypes. At first, in this chapter we are going to work with bars. They have open, low, high, and close prices. We should define timestamps and time intervals. A conversion to day duration is quite useful for further volatility annualizing, that is, casting to volatility in one year interval. This is found in `BarTypes.hs`.

Also we add the derivations of common instances `Eq`, `Show`, and `Enum`. Please note that we did not define `duration _`, because if function is not defined on some of `BarType`, the compiler running with the `-Wall` option will produce the warning. For example, if the line with `Bar4Hours` is commented, then the compiler will warn you:

```
$ ghc BarTypes.hs -Wall
[1 of 1] Compiling BarType          ( BarTypes.hs, BarTypes.o )

BarTypes.hs:16:1: Warning:
    Pattern match(es) are non-exhaustive
    In an equation for `duration': Patterns not matched: Bar4Hours
```

This allows us to be sure that all the possible values of bar type and corresponding execution paths are considered in the definition of the `duration` function.

The trivial definition of bar type can be found in `Bar.hs`.

As we would like to write high performance code, we should understand that as most of garbage-collecting language runtimes, Haskell Runtime System (RTS) provides boxing of primitive types, that is, an integer becomes an object inside the runtime thus enabling reference counting and freeing, though, for high performance calculation it is better to avoid such situations. Unfortunately, the compiler is not that smart to automatically avoid boxing, even if it tries in many scenarios. Usually it is better to provide an `UNPACK` hint to the compiler as given in `BarOptimized.hs`.

Also we should recall that Haskell is a language with lazy computations, that is, it tries to defer computations as much as possible. In case of time series process this might make a huge overhead by creating a lot of deferred computations until the final result is retrieved. To avoid such cases, strictness annotation, exclamation mark `!` exists in the language. It forces the compiler to ensure that the field is fully evaluated before passing the value to the constructor. However, one should know that it might make the performance worse because if it turns out that the field has already been evaluated, then all those evaluations will be just wasted. Of course, the compiler might guess and remove such wasted computations but currently GHC does a poor job and it cannot guess if the functions used for field computations are the same or not, even if they are pure. Therefore, it just relies on the proper naming of function results. To clarify the difference let's take a look at the example, `TT.hs`.

The first function evaluates `x + 1` twice, one for each field of TT but the second function does this evaluation only once.

Next we should define an estimator interface as the following type class. In fact, input is just a list of bars and output is volatility of `Estimators.hs`.

The `algorithm` type class parameter defines the algorithm used for estimation. Now we are ready to make a first step and implement the simple volatility estimator in `Simple.hs`.

Here we reuse the `statistics` package to compute the standard deviation of the sample with mean.

Alternative volatility estimators

Though the volatility definition is pretty simple, it has a major drawback. It is a very poor estimate for small sample sizes. If the underlying process is log normal, then variance of the estimated variance is given approximately as follows:

$$VarVarX \approx \frac{\sigma^2}{2N}$$

So using more data we would get a closer estimate of the true process. Even if it is completely fine for stationary, unchanging processes, it is quite problematic for financial markets. If we use very less data, then our estimate is quite noisy. Using too much data gives an estimate irrelevant to the current market state. Choosing the right balance is quite an art and it is hard to formalize it to an algorithm.

There are two basic ways to address the large sampling error problem. We can use higher-frequency data or we can construct another estimator that either uses all available observations or uses derivative prices. We always can feed the algorithm with more fine data and possibly get the better results but this is valid only till some point, so let us first study alternative algorithms that use more advanced approaches and yield better volatility estimates.

The Parkinson's number

The first estimator was developed by *Parkinson* in 1980 to estimate the volatility of returns for Geometric Brownian Motion using the high and low prices at any particular period:

$$\sigma_p = \sqrt{\frac{1}{4N\log 2}\sum_{i=1}^{N}\left(\log\frac{h_i}{l_i}\right)^2}$$

Here $h_i\left(l_i\right)$ is a high (low) price in the time interval. Such an estimator is only applicable to the aggregated time interval, that is, when the range exists. Otherwise, for points we get $h_i = l_i$ and therefore, $\sigma = 0$. Also it highlights one of its biggest drawbacks – systematic underestimation of volatility. Moreover, it cannot deal with jumps and trends and this estimator is really appropriate only for measuring volatility of the Geometric Brownian Motion. The Parkinson number is about five time more efficient in comparison with the simple estimator. Thus you will need approximately five time less data points to achieve the same variance of the estimate. Also it makes perfect sense that the range of a trading interval defines volatility of that interval.

Haskell implementation is pretty trivial but there is a trick to enforce strictness as in `Parkinson.hs`.

Here we define an internal datatype `T` with enforced strictness and unpacking just to be sure that the inner loop of estimator calculation will be executed in place and without boxing. In general, it makes sense to mark accumulator as strict in the list folds as its values will be needed at the end of computation.

The Garman-Klass estimator

The other type of estimator is a family of Garman-Klass estimators. They are all well described in a paper by *Mark B. Garman and Michael J. Klass* (`http://www.fea.com/resources/pdf/a_estimation_of_security_price.pdf`). Their practical recommendation is to use the "fifth" estimator as follows:

$$\sigma = \sqrt{\frac{1}{2N}\sum_{i=1}^{N}\left(log\frac{h_i}{l_i}\right)^2 - \frac{2log2-1}{N}\sum_{i=1}^{N}\left(log\frac{c_i}{o_i}\right)^2}$$

It is the most effective estimator of this family and is up to eight times better than close-to-close one, and this estimator uses nearly all the information available from the market. If we compare it with the Parkinson estimator, we will find that it is even more biased towards volatility underestimation.

The implementation of `GarmanKlass.hs` is pretty straightforward and just follows the formula with addition of strictness annotations to TT just like we did with T.

The Rogers-Satchel estimator

The major assumption of the estimators already discussed is that market follows drift-less **Geometric Brownian Motion (GBM)** and it doesn't apply to markets all the time. An estimator, that outperforms the others in the presence of drift has been developed by *Rogers*, *Satchel*, and *Yoon* and is as follows:

$$\sigma = \sqrt{\frac{1}{N}\sum_{i=1}^{N}\left[log\frac{h_i}{c_i}log\frac{h_i}{o_i} + log\frac{l_i}{c_i}log\frac{l_i}{o_i}\right]}$$

It cannot deal with jumps as all previous estimators. Haskell implementation just follows the formula by implementing the estimator instance in `Rogers.hs`.

The Yang-Zhang estimator

This estimator tries to solve the problem of trends and jumps. In fact, the Yang-Zhang estimator is a weighed average of unbiased variances of open and close log prices and the Rogers-Satchels estimator:

$$\sigma = \sqrt{\sigma_0^2 + k\sigma_c^2 + (1-k)\sigma_{rs}^2}$$

Here

$$\sigma_0^2 = Varlogo = \frac{1}{N-1}\sum_{i=1}^{N}\left(logo_i - logo'\right)^2$$

$$\sigma_c^2 = Varlogc = \frac{1}{N-1}\sum_{i=1}^{N}\left(logc_i - logc'\right)^2$$

$$\sigma_{rs}^2 = \frac{1}{N}\sum_{i=1}^{N}\left[log\frac{h_i}{c_i}log\frac{h_i}{o_i} + log\frac{l_i}{c_i}log\frac{l_i}{o_i}\right]$$

$$k = \frac{0.34}{1.34 + \frac{N+1}{N-1}}$$

The performance of this estimator significantly degrades if the process is close to pure jumps.

Choosing a volatility estimator

Now we have six estimators in hand and the question is how to choose the proper estimator. Unfortunately this question doesn't have a simple answer. Each estimator gives some piece of valuable information. For instance, if Parkinson volatility is twice as much as close-to-close volatility, then, most probably, the true volatility is driven by large intraday movements and those closing prices will just cover them. But in general, it is a kind of art to choose an appropriate estimator for given market conditions.

The variation ratio method

Variance ratio is computed by dividing the variance of returns estimated from longer intervals by the variance of returns estimated from shorter intervals (for the same measurement period), and then normalizing this value to one by dividing it by the ratio of the longer interval to the shorter interval. A variance ratio that is greater than one suggests that the returns series is serially correlated positively or that the shorter interval returns a trend within the duration of the longer interval. A variance ratio that is less than one suggests that the return series is serially correlated negatively or that the shorter interval returns and tends towards the mean reversion within the duration of the longer interval as shown in the following table:

Annualized volatilities of year 2010

Currency pair	By minute	By hour	By 4 hours	By day
EUR/USD	12.28%	11.71%	12.02%	12.14%
USD/CHF	12.87%	11.64%	11.61%	10.75%
EUR/CHF	10.25%	9.06%	8.86%	9.23%
GBP/USD	11.87%	11.03%	11.11%	10.08%
EUR/GBP	11.03%	9.54%	9.80%	9.52%

So, we might conclude that USD/CHF and GBP/USD have some mean-reverting property during the day, others are mean-reverting only in an hour time frame.

Parkinson number of year 2010

Currency pair	By minute	By hours	By 4 hours	By day
EUR/USD	8.72%	11.36%	11.63%	11.72%
USD/CHF	9.05%	11.56%	11.72%	11.30%
EUR/CHF	7.04%	8.95%	8.99%	8.96%
GBP/USD	8.52%	10.89%	10.99%	10.08%
EUR/GBP	7.93%	9.46%	9.63%	9.83%

For Geometric Brownian Motion, we can define the Parkinson-to-volatility ratio:

$$\frac{\sigma_p}{\sigma} \approx 1.67$$

Deviation from this value shows how much the process deviates from GBM. As we can see in our results, currency pairs deviate significantly from GBM.

Forecasting volatility

Besides estimation, volatility forecasting is the next big task in trading. It is obviously a hard task that nobody has solved and won't be able to solve but we can make some estimates and bets in future. So, in fact, we might predict an approximate form of volatility distribution.

One such method lies in the observation that prices exhibit time volatility clustering. There are periods of high volatility, swings followed by calm times. In other words, time series has a memory effect in volatility, therefore, the first approach is to split return residuals into a stochastic piece z_t and a time-dependent deviation σ_t:

$$r_t - r' = \sigma_t z_t$$

The random variable z_t is white noise. And the volatility series σ_t is modeled as:

$$\sigma_t^2 = \omega + \sum_{i=1}^{q} \alpha_i \left(r_{t-i} - r'\right)^2$$

This model is called the Autoregressive Conditional Heteroskedasticity model of rank q, $ARCH(q)$. As we are working with log returns, we can omit r' because it is usually about zero and thus simplifies formulas and reasoning about the model.

In fact, we can also include an autoregressive moving average model for variances into ARCH and get a generalized autoregressive conditional heteroskedasticity model, GARCH. If p is the order of the variance term and q is the order of the ARCH terms, then the model is given as follows:

$$\sigma_t^2 = \omega + \sum_{i=1}^{q} \alpha_i \gamma_{t-i}^2 + \sum_{i=1}^{p} \beta_i \sigma_{t-i}^2$$

Here and further we will study GARCH(1,1) for the sake of simplicity.

The GARCH (1,1) model

There is another way to express the model by splitting the constant term ω into a long-term variance V and a scaling constant γ as follows:

$$\sigma_t^2 = \gamma V + \alpha r_{t-1}^2 + \beta \sigma_{t-1}^2$$

Given the amount of information about the GARCH model we might capture it in Haskell types as in `Garch.hs`.

Here we introduce a `MarketState` function to capture the current state of the market that is in fact a pair of return r_t and variance σ_t^2. The `Garch11` datatype just keeps all the parameters of the GARCH(1,1) model.

Now we can construct a single-step prediction by using the `forecast` function. Also we provided a function, `buildVariance` that builds variance series by starting volatility and return series for the given model. The `scanl` function is quite useful and its informal definition is quite simple (in pseudo-Haskell) and is found in `Scanl.hs`.

This function is a variation of fold that records all the intermediate values into the output array.

Maximum likelihood estimation of parameters

As discussed in the previous chapter, to estimate parameters by MLE, we form a joint probability density function as a function of parameters, given the data and maximize the likelihood function with respect to the parameters.

If the returns were independently distributed from each other, we could write the function as the product of marginal densities, but in the GARCH model they are not independent. However, it is possible to write it as the following product:

$$
\begin{aligned}
f(r_1, r_2, \ldots, r_N) = & \quad f(r_N \mid r_1, r_2, \ldots, r_{N-1}) f(r_1, r_2, \ldots, r_{N-1}) \\
= & \quad f(r_N \mid r_1, r_2, \ldots, r_{N-1}) f(r_N \mid r_1, r_2, \ldots, r_{N-2}) f(r_1, r_2, \ldots, r_{N-2}) \\
= & \quad f(r_N \mid r_1, r_2, \ldots, r_{N-1}) f(r_N \mid r_1, r_2, \ldots, r_{N-2}) \cdots f(r_1)
\end{aligned}
$$

Obviously an additional assumption should be put on the conditional distribution of returns to calibrate the model. Let's start with the usual assumption of normal returns. Thus the likelihood function becomes as follows:

$$
L = \prod_{i=1}^{N} \frac{1}{\sqrt{2\pi\sigma_i^2}} exp\left(\frac{-(r_i - \mu)^2}{2\sigma_i^2} \right)
$$

So far we can maximize a log-likelihood function as L is a monotonically increasing function:

$$
logL = \frac{-N}{2} log 2\pi - \frac{1}{2}\sum_{i=1}^{N} \sigma_i^2 - \frac{1}{2}\sum_{i=1}^{N} \frac{(r_i - \mu)^2}{\sigma_i^2}
$$

And for GARCH we should substitute $\sigma_i^2 = \gamma V + \alpha r_{i-1}^2 + \beta\sigma_{i-1}^2$ into the preceding equation and the log-likelihood becomes a function of the returns and the parameters. Notice that we should also estimate V and σ_1.

Implementation details

Let's summarize how the log-likelihood function should be calculated:

1. Take a logarithm of returns: $r_i = log \frac{x_i}{x_{i-1}}$.
2. Calculate the mean (μ) of log-returns.
3. For the given α, β, γ, V and σ_1^2 construct a series of GARCH σ_t^2.
4. Using all the preceding values calculate the log-likelihood

The first two steps are good candidates for precalculation and we give them as input parameters into the `logLikelihood` function, whereas the third and fourth steps require a more elaborate approach as given in `LogGarch.hs`.

In the `LogGarch.hs` file, you can see that we used the `INLINE` pragma. Though that might be quite useful optimization, it should be applied carefully. By default, GHC tries to inline or to "unfold" functions and values that are small enough to avoid call overhead and possibly to expose to more sophisticated optimization of inlined code. The pragma says that this function is cheap enough to be inlined. But GHC will inline only "fully applied" functions, that is, taking as many arguments that appear on the left-hand side of the function's definition. Therefore, if we like to use the `logLikelihood` function in a partially applied form, that is, when input prices are known and we are optimizing the parameters of cost function as follows:

```
costFunction :: Double -> Garch11 -> Double
costFunction = logLikelihood rs
```

In this case, GHC won't inline the function definition here and produce the ordinary call. To make it inlineable we make the following transformations without semantic changes:

```
logLikelihood :: U.Vector Double -> Double -> Garch11 -> Double
logLikelihood rs = \s0 g ->
    let
        n                   = fromIntegral $ U.length rs
        mu                  = mean rs
        variances           = buildVolatilities g s0 rs
        sumOfVariance       = U.sum variances
        sumOfResidues       = U.foldl' (residue mu) 0.0 $ U.zip rs
variances
        residue m a (r, s) = a + (r - m) ** 2 / s
    in
        - 0.5*(n*log2pi + sumOfVariance + sumOfResidues)
{-# INLINE logLikelihood #-}
```

So now the method returns the lambda function and thus the compiler can embed it into the usage point. Though the HLint might complain by throwing the "Redundant lambda" error, this is a necessary complication of the function.

Parallel computations

Till now we did not mention any parallelization of Haskell program. Fortunately this is something that goes along with data immutability and pure functions. As parallelism and concurrency are usually misused for not-the-same things, let's define parallelism as a set of techniques to run a program faster by performing several computations in parallel. This usually requires additional hardware units (multi-core CPUs). Concurrency, on the other hand, is a set of techniques to make the program more useable, for example, to spin off a thread to accomplish the background query to a web service or something similar to this.

If we consider an imperative language in parallel computations, the usual types of bugs are concurrent, non-synchronized, and writes to memory. Haskell immutable data might be accessed from any thread without even the theoretical possibility of memory corruption or access to stale data. Immutability provides quite a nice feature of referential transparency, that is, an expression can be replaced with its value without changing the program behavior. This helps in algorithm simplification, correctness proofs, and optimizations by means of memorization and common subexpression elimination.

Parallelization also benefits from referential transparency. GHC can reason about the program flow and reason about computation parallelization if it is required or needed. Though, it would be a killer feature if GHC could do parallelization automatically; it is a very hard task and has not been solved yet. So the compiler still requires explicit hints for parallelization.

Code benchmarking

Before getting into optimization it would be great to have a reliable measurement of performance. As *Donald Knuth* said:

> *Premature optimization is the root of all evil.*

Therefore, we should be confident that the program gets benefits from parallelization and optimization.

There is a sophisticated benchmarking library, `criterion`, which can be installed as usually by `cabal`:

```
$ cabal install criterion
```

The library defines a convenient, default main function that does all the benchmarking. Let's take a look at a simple example in `Criterion.hs`.

Once it is compiled with `ghc -O --make Criterion.hs`, we can run it and get a report similar to the following one:

```
> ./Criterion
warming up
estimating clock resolution...
mean is 3.535129 us (160001 iterations)
found 1410 outliers among 159999 samples (0.9%)
  1302 (0.8%) high severe
estimating cost of a clock call...
mean is 118.1560 ns (35 iterations)
found 7 outliers among 35 samples (20.0%)
  1 (2.9%) high mild
  6 (17.1%) high severe

benchmarking factorial 100
mean: 12.63666 us, lb 12.55126 us, ub 12.86132 us, ci 0.950
std dev: 662.3861 ns, lb 316.8517 ns, ub 1.399939 us, ci 0.950
found 7 outliers among 100 samples (7.0%)
  5 (5.0%) high mild
  2 (2.0%) high severe
variance introduced by outliers: 50.462%
variance is severely inflated by outliers
```

We can see that the library takes a lot of efforts to provide consistent and significant results of benchmarking. It provides a bootstrapping technique to estimate the accuracy of the benchmark and makes clock accuracy correction.

The library defines the `defaultMain` function that drives all the benchmarking process. The bench function creates a benchmark object that provides a specification of future measurements that might be either a pure computation represented by the `Pure` datatype, or the typical `IO` monad for an impure one.

The function name, `whnf` stands for **Weak Head Normal Form** (**WHNF**), which is approximately a synonym for Haskell lazy computation. As we already mentioned in the previous chapters, Haskell doesn't evaluate expressions until it is really needed. Evaluation to WHNF computes only to the most outermost constructor, that is, it just creates a value but put inside only a promise to compute the value at the moment when it is retrieved. Such promise is usually called a `thunk`, a special object with input arguments and a function to be computed. Thus if the constructor is not strict in its arguments, evaluation to WHNF returns just an empty object with a thunk inside it. Therefore one should be quite careful not to measure object creation.

In fact, criterion library can force a value and reduce the benchmarking function to the normal form using the `nf` function.

Haskell Run-Time System

Before starting with parallel code in Haskell, we should understand the core of Haskell execution, Haskell Run-Time System (RTS). GHC provides the core RTS that includes everything required to execute the Haskell code:

- Storage manager with multi-generational garbage collector
- Byte code interpreter for GHCi
- Heap and time-profiler with code coverage support
- Software transaction memory support
- User-space scheduler of Haskell threads

Haskell threads are a sort of lightweight threads that are placed on top of the OS-supported threads. And there are two different approaches to manage them: either schedule all of them on a single OS thread, or split to several OS threads. These two approaches differ drastically in complexity and overheads. The second approach might introduce quite a significant overhead into a simple program but the parallel and/or concurrent program can benefit significantly from it. This is the reason for having two types of RTS: simple or non-threaded, and threaded.

By default, GHC generates a single-threaded code, even if it is written with parallel markers. To enable a multi-threaded RTS it should be explicitly chosen at link time by the `-threaded` option.

The divide-and-conquer approach

The factorial function, which we will see, is not written for parallelization. It uses a tail recursion and therefore, each step of the algorithm depends on the previous one, but for effective parallelization, the algorithm should allow two or more parallel streams. There is an important algorithm design paradigm – the divide and conquer approach. Such an algorithm should work by recursively breaking down a problem into two subproblems of the same type and the solutions to the subproblems are combined to get a solution to the original problem. Mathematically we can express it in the following form:

$$f(a \cup b) = g(a) \otimes g(b)$$

Factorial can be rewritten in a non-recursive way as follows:

```
factorial :: Integer -> Integer
factorial 0 = 1
factorial 1 = 1
factorial n = product [1..n]
```

Measurement of performance of such definitions gives us slightly worse numbers than a recursive version.

```
warming up
estimating clock resolution...
mean is 2.512470 us (320001 iterations)
found 3223 outliers among 319999 samples (1.0%)
  2904 (0.9%) high severe
estimating cost of a clock call...
mean is 98.36037 ns (17 iterations)
found 1 outliers among 17 samples (5.9%)
  1 (5.9%) high mild

benchmarking factorial 100
mean: 13.99081 us, lb 13.71873 us, ub 14.71319 us, ci 0.950
std dev: 2.121902 us, lb 984.2068 ns, ub 4.483487 us, ci 0.950
found 8 outliers among 100 samples (8.0%)
  4 (4.0%) high mild
  4 (4.0%) high severe
variance introduced by outliers: 90.437%
variance is severely inflated by outliers
```

As far as multiplication of integers is commutative and transitive, we can rewrite the built-in `product` function with multi-branched recursion. We will split the array in the middle all the time until it is not empty:

```
parProduct :: Num a => [a] -> a
parProduct [] = 1
parProduct [x] = x
parProduct xs = left*right
    where
        n = length xs `div` 2
        (leftL, rightL) = splitAt n xs
        left = parProduct leftL
        right = parProduct rightL
```

Here we can see that an empty list is a group unit in the list datatype. And the following results are not even close to the best one:

```
benchmarking factorial 100
mean: 33.00396 us, lb 32.43377 us, ub 33.75064 us, ci 0.950
std dev: 3.341864 us, lb 2.714208 us, ub 4.204187 us, ci 0.950
```

Next, we are going to see what will happen if we create too many sublists. Start by compiling the program with the `-rtsopts` option that enables a lot of debugging options for the program and then by running with the `+RTS -s` option. These options print out the garbage collector statistics as follows:

```
   2,629,606,024 bytes allocated in the heap
       5,558,712 bytes copied during GC
       5,228,944 bytes maximum residency (109 sample(s))
       1,725,760 bytes maximum slop
              11 MB total memory in use (1 MB lost due to fragmentation)

                                    Tot time (elapsed)  Avg pause  Max
pause
  Gen  0      4963 colls,     0 par    0.04s    0.05s     0.0000s
0.0006s
  Gen  1       109 colls,     0 par    0.04s    0.04s     0.0004s
0.0016s

  INIT    time    0.00s  (  0.00s elapsed)
  MUT     time    3.61s  (  4.04s elapsed)
  GC      time    0.07s  (  0.09s elapsed)
  EXIT    time    0.00s  (  0.00s elapsed)
  Total   time    3.68s  (  4.13s elapsed)
```

```
%GC     time       2.0%  (2.2% elapsed)

Alloc rate    728,913,779 bytes per MUT second

Productivity  98.0% of total user, 87.4% of total elapsed
```

Garbage collection doesn't seem to be a problem in this algorithm as it takes only 2 percent of the whole running time. But the total allocation is about 2.5 GB and it allocates about 700 MB per MUT second. GHC measures different times of program run. `INIT` is the runtime system initialization, `MUT` is the "mutator time", that is, the time of actual code run. `GC` is the garbage collector time. `EXIT` is the runtime system shutdown time. The only reasonable way to minimize allocation rate is to limit a recursion depth.

Now we annotate the multi-branched code of factorial with parallelism functions `par` and `pseq` as follows:

```
parProduct :: Num a => [a] -> a
parProduct [] = 1
parProduct [x] = x
parProduct xs = left `par` (right `pseq` (right * left))
    where
        n = length xs `div` 2
        (leftL, rightL) = splitAt n xs
        left = parProduct leftL
        right = parProduct rightL
```

The main function definition says that it might be good to compute the `left` variable in parallel. The second part says that at first, strictly, we need the `right` variable and then it should return multiplication of `left` and `right`. As we said earlier, the code should be compiled with the `-threaded` option and run with `+RTS -N`. The output should be as follows:

```
benchmarking factorial 100
mean: 20.23398 us, lb 19.22427 us, ub 21.75845 us, ci 0.950
std dev: 6.298791 us, lb 4.462945 us, ub 8.295099 us, ci 0.950
```

Thus we get from 33 ms to 20 ms, that is, it runs 1.65 times faster which is not bad but the ideal speed up should be two times faster. In this simple example the cost of sparking parallel computations seems to be pretty high.

The par function doesn't really guarantee that the expression will be evaluated in parallel with another. It is just a hint for RTS to decide to spark a parallel computation. The circumstances affecting the decision might include current load and "heaviness" of the computation. For instance, if all CPU cores are busy, then RTS might go with sequential execution to avoid a new thread creation. This flexibility affects the way parallel code can be written. In fact, if RTS is quite intelligent, we might put the par annotation anywhere.

GARCH code in parallel

Having taken a look at the logLikelihood function in the LogGarch module we might notice that sumOfVariance and sumOfResidues can be computed in parallel.

```
logLikelihood :: U.Vector Double -> Double -> Garch11 -> Double
logLikelihood rs s0 g =
    let
        n                    = fromIntegral $ U.length rs
        mu                   = mean rs
        variances            = buildVolatilities g s0 rs
        sumOfVariance        = U.sum variances
        sumOfResidues        = U.foldl' (residue mu) 0.0 $ U.zip rs
variances
        residue m a (r, s) = a + (r - m) ** 2 / s
    in
        variances `pseq` (sumOfVariance `par` (sumOfResidues `pseq`
            (- 0.5*(n*log2pi + sumOfVariance + sumOfResidues))))
```

We should annotate variances with sequential execution to avoid double computation of the same variable.

Evaluation strategy

The par and pseq functions can introduce the same level of clutter as does thread communication in imperative programming. Therefore, it would be great to separate algorithm and evaluation. First, we need to deal with Haskell's laziness and be able to force argument evaluation up to normal form. A class of types NFData has been added to cope with the fully evaluated data. NFData stands for normal form data. Its definition includes only the rnf function, that is, reduce to NF.

```
class NFData a where
   rnf :: a -> ()
```

This type class is defined for all main Haskell types, including lists and tuples. For user-defined types we might need to define it.

Generalization of this approach is an evaluation strategy that doesn't perform any computation on a value but just ensures that a value is evaluated to some extent. And the `Control.Parallel.Strategies` module defines the `Strategy` type as follows:

```
type Strategy a = a -> Eval a
```

By convention the `Strategy` function may do an arbitrary amount of evaluation of its argument but will not return a value different from the one it was passed with.

The module defines the following basic strategies:

- `r0` performs no evaluation
- `rseq` evaluates to WHNF
- `rdeepseq` evaluates to NF
- `rpar` sparks its argument for evaluation in parallel

Combination of these four basic strategies generates all other possible evaluation strategies. The most useful ones, such as parallel map (`parMap`), parallel traverse (`parTraverse`), and parallel list (`parList`), are defined in `Control.Parallel.Strategies`.

In this approach we might specify `parProduct` by just marking what we want to be evaluated in parallel right now:

```
parProduct :: Num a => [a] -> a
parProduct [] = 1
parProduct [x] = x
parProduct xs = (right `using` rpar) * left
    where
        n = length xs `div` 2
        (leftL, rightL) = splitAt n xs
        left = product leftL
        right = product rightL
```

For associative operators, for example, multiplication, it is possible to write a parallel fold as follows:

```
parFold :: Strategy a -> (a -> a -> a) -> a -> [a] -> a
parFold strat f = foldl (\ z x -> f z x `using` strat)
```

And using this function, `parProduct` simplifies to `parFold r0 (*) 1`.

Summary

In this chapter, we discussed the volatility prediction model GARCH. As we saw, the GARCH model doesn't pose any kind of restrictions on the underlying distributions, thus giving the first point of extension. The normal distribution used before doesn't describe heavy tails of returns' distribution. The next obvious extension point is a form of polynomial. This point generates an infinite family of models.

Also in the chapter we discussed a deterministic parallelism in Haskell. We built a parallel factorial toy function and got a glimpse of parallel GARCH implementation.

6
Advanced Cabal

Any project having more than a couple of files requires a build system, unit testing, dependency management, and documentation, otherwise it cracks under its own heaviness. The rule of thumb that was brought by the test-driven development approach is that the build and test cycle should be easy and run fast, otherwise nobody will use intermediate builds and tests. Ideally all these processes should be automated.

Haskell addresses these problems by providing the **Common Architecture for Building Applications and Libraries** (CABAL). The tool is used to:

- Build the project
- Manage dependencies of the project
- Run tests and benchmarks
- Generate documentation
- Work with common repository of packages (Hackage)

The tool is in continuous development and the latest release 1.18.0 brought hermetic builds with sandbox and support for GHCi REPL inside sandbox.

Cabal can install packages into one of the following predefined places:

- Global repository that is available for all users. This happens if you use an OS package manager, or if you install it with Cabal either as root/administrator or with the `--global` option.
- User's repository in the user's home directory. Such packages are available only for that user and it is a default behavior of Cabal.
- Sandboxed in a project specific directory. It makes packages available only within the scope of the project.

Common usage

As we mentioned already the common usage of Cabal is package installation using the following command:

```
cabal install <pkg-name>
```

Successful execution of this command installs the package into the user's repository of Haskell packages. Right after that, the package can be linked to and used by any Haskell program. The package discovery relies on Hackage (`http://hackage.haskell.org`), the common repository of packages. For proper functioning before the first run of Cabal we require to run an `update` command that downloads the list of all available packages with their respective metadata:

```
cabal update
```

It is recommended to run `update` periodically to get a fresh list of packages from Hackage. On a Unix-like system it might be a good idea to set up a cron to run such update automatically.

Packaging with Cabal

To start with creating a new package in Cabal, you should run an interactive wizard using the following command:

```
cabal init
```

Cabal will ask you the package name, version, license, author name, author's e-mail ID, package synopsis, category, library or executable build target, and other minor parameters. By using these inputs, the tool will create a Cabal file and the `Setup.hs` file. The approximate content of an automatically generated Cabal file is is shown in the `test.cabal` file.

You should set up `hs-source-dirs` to point to the directory with Haskell sources and because this package provides a library, the list of exposed modules (`exposed-modules`) are also required. Internal modules should be specified in the `other-modules` section. To make a first build of the library you should run, configure, and build steps using the following commands:

```
cabal configure
cabal build
```

At the `configure` step, Cabal checks if all the project dependencies are satisfied. Then at the `build` step it will produce required artifacts (libraries or executables). The `Setup.hs` file allows customization of build process that might be required in case of complex libraries and executables with requirements to build third-party libraries written in other languages. The `Simple` build is more than enough for usual Haskell development. According to the build description, it is not called `Simple` because it is simple, but "because it does complicated things to a simple software". The autogenerated `Setup.hs` file is very short:

```
import Distribution.Simple
main = defaultMain
```

This default `main` function provides all the functionalities of Cabal. To add the test suite into the project, the following lines should be appended to the Cabal project:

```
test-suite  basic
    type: exitcode-stdio-1.0
    main-is: tests/basic-test.hs
    build-depends:   base >=4.6 && <4.7
```

Here we specified the type of test suite, `exitcode-stdio-1.0`. Such test suites rely on the exit code of execution of the script from `main-is`. To run the test suite, the project must be configured with the tests enabled as follows:

```
cabal configure --enable-tests
cabal build
cabal test
```

It will run all the test suites defined in the Cabal file and print their output on to the standard output. There is also an other type of test suite, `detailed-1.0`, but it doesn't seem to be very well supported. Cabal also provides the `clean` command that removes all artifacts generated by the `build` system.

Cabal in sandbox

Cabal, by default, installs all packages to the user package repository. Though it keeps track of the package version, this does not eliminate a Cabal dependency hell. Let's say if an application A requires a library B of Version 2.0 and reuses a library C that requires the library B of Version 1.0. This immediately violates a GHC rule of single package version per build as B should be comprised of both the versions and the build fails with the "Could not resolve dependencies" error. And over the time, with installation of new packages and upgradation of the old ones, this situation becomes more and more likely.

One of the easiest and fastest solutions is to reset all the packages on the system by deleting all the `cabal` and `ghc-pkg` caches. For instance, on a Unix-like system one can run the following cleanup:

```
rm -rf ~/.ghc ~/.cabal/lib ~/.cabal/share ~/.cabal/packages
```

It is an easy fix, but still two projects may interfere with each other's dependencies, and we will be back into Cabal dependency hell.

Another approach is to build and manage dependencies separately for each project, in other words, it creates a sandbox for a project. There were a lot of attempts made to provide a toolset for it, and most prominent tools are `cabal-dev`, `virtualhenv`, and `hsenv`. The first tool provides a sandboxed Cabal that installs dependencies into the project's local directory and, thus, does not pollute the user package repository. The `Hsenv` and `virtualhenv` projects have got their inspiration from Python's `virtualenv` project and they allow to "sandbox" a whole tool chain, from compiler to packages.

Starting from version 1.18.0, Cabal supports sandboxing without additional tools. The usage of sandbox is quite simple: once you initialize a fresh sandbox, all further Cabal commands will be executed inside the box. The typical usage is as follows:

```
cabal sandbox init
cabal install --only-dependencies
cabal build
```

This set of commands initializes a new sandbox, installs dependencies, and makes a full build of the project. It will create a configuration file, `cabal.sandbox.config` and a cache directory, `.cabal-sandbox` to keep the already built packages.

Another frequent version of dependency hell is when a package depends on different versions of the same package. To resolve such problems, you should modify Cabal files and/or the code of some of the intermediate packages. In such cases you can reference the source code of those packages inside your project. Also it might be useful if you need to build with another project in development. In that case, the following `add-source` command will help:

```
cabal sandbox add-source <path to library>
cabal install --dependencies-only
cabal build
```

Now Cabal will track changes of the library in the path and in case of changes the dependency will also be rebuilt.

Cabal also provides a way to start GHCi within the sandbox by using the following command:

```
cabal repl
```

This command will use the first component in the package. If you require to run GHCi REPL command within another component of the package, you can run with its name as follows:

```
cabal repl basic
```

This loads a basic test suite into GHCi with its dependencies.

Summary

In this chapter we went through the Haskell package management system, Cabal, and took a look at its main features such as building, testing, and sandboxing.

References

For further language and platform reference, you can use the following resources:

- *Haskell 2010 Language Report*: http://www.haskell.org/onlinereport/haskell2010/
- *Real World Haskell by Bryan O'Sullivan, Don Stewart, and John Goerzen*: http://book.realworldhaskell.org/
- *Learn You a Haskell for Great Good!* by *Miran Lipovača* (http://learnyouahaskell.com/)
- Introduction to Functional Programming using Haskell by *Richard Bird*
- Pearls of Functional Algorithm Design by *Richard Bird*
- School of Expression by *Paul Hudak*
- The Craft of Haskell by *Graham Hutton*
- *Homotopy Type Theory: Univalent Foundations of Mathematics*: http://homotopytypetheory.org/book/
- *Cabal User Guide*: http://www.haskell.org/cabal/users-guide/
- Cabal sandbox: http://coldwa.st/e/blog/2013-08-20-Cabal-sandbox.html

The financial and mathematical part of this book is mostly inspired by the following works:

- Dynamic Hedging: Managing Vanilla and Exotic Options by *Nassim Nicholas Taleb*
- Monte Carlo Methods in Finance by *Peter Jaeckel*
- Handbook of Statistical Analysis and Data Mining Application by *Robert Nisbet, John Elder IV*, and *Gary Miner*
- Econometrics of Financial High-Frequency Data by *Nikolaus Hautsch*

- Handbook of Modeling High-Frequency Data in Finance, edited by *Viens*, *Mariani*, and *Florescu*
- Monte Carlo Methods in Financial Engineering (Stochastic Modelling and Applied Probability) by *Paul Glasserman*
- Algorithmic Trading and DMA, an introduction to direct access strategies by *Barry Johnson*
- Volatility Trading by *Euan Sinclair*
- The Evaluation and Optimization of Trading Strategies by *Robert Pardo*
- The Encyclopedia of Trading Strategies by *Jeffrey Owen Katz*, Ph.D. and *Donna L. McCormik*

Index

Symbols

A

B

C

[PACKT] open source
community experience distilled
PUBLISHING

Thank you for buying
Haskell Financial Data Modeling and Predictive Analytics

About Packt Publishing

Packt, pronounced 'packed', published its first book "*Mastering phpMyAdmin for Effective MySQL Management*" in April 2004 and subsequently continued to specialize in publishing highly focused books on specific technologies and solutions.

Our books and publications share the experiences of your fellow IT professionals in adapting and customizing today's systems, applications, and frameworks. Our solution based books give you the knowledge and power to customize the software and technologies you're using to get the job done. Packt books are more specific and less general than the IT books you have seen in the past. Our unique business model allows us to bring you more focused information, giving you more of what you need to know, and less of what you don't.

Packt is a modern, yet unique publishing company, which focuses on producing quality, cutting-edge books for communities of developers, administrators, and newbies alike. For more information, please visit our website: `www.packtpub.com`.

About Packt Open Source

In 2010, Packt launched two new brands, Packt Open Source and Packt Enterprise, in order to continue its focus on specialization. This book is part of the Packt Open Source brand, home to books published on software built around Open Source licences, and offering information to anybody from advanced developers to budding web designers. The Open Source brand also runs Packt's Open Source Royalty Scheme, by which Packt gives a royalty to each Open Source project about whose software a book is sold.

Writing for Packt

We welcome all inquiries from people who are interested in authoring. Book proposals should be sent to author@packtpub.com. If your book idea is still at an early stage and you would like to discuss it first before writing a formal book proposal, contact us; one of our commissioning editors will get in touch with you.

We're not just looking for published authors; if you have strong technical skills but no writing experience, our experienced editors can help you develop a writing career, or simply get some additional reward for your expertise.

[PACKT] PUBLISHING open source
community experience distilled

Statistical Analysis with R Beginner's Guide

ISBN: 978-1-84951-208-4 Paperback: 300 pages

Take control of your data and produce superior statistical analyses with R

1. An easy introduction for people who are new to R, with plenty of strong examples for you to work through
2. This book will take you on a journey to learn R as the strategist for an ancient Chinese kingdom!
3. An easy introduction for people who are new to R, with plenty of strong examples for you to work through

---

BIRT 2.6 Data Analysis and Reporting

ISBN: 978-1-84951-166-7 Paperback: 360 pages

Create, design, format, and deploy reports with the world's most popular Eclipse-based Business Intelligence and Reporting Tool

1. Design, manage, format, and deploy high-quality reports
2. Crosstab reports using the new BIRT cube designer
3. Transform raw data into visual and interactive reports
4. Includes a case study (Building Reports for Bugzilla) at the end along with a real-world example that runs throughout the book

Please check **www.PacktPub.com** for information on our titles

27870231R10062

Made in the USA
Lexington, KY
26 November 2013